The Art of Lecturing

The Art of Lecturing

Six lectures by

Rudolf Steiner

Dornach, October 11-16, 1921

MERCURY PRESS

This edition of: *The Art of Lecturing*,
first published by Mercury Press in 1984,
is a compilation of translations that have appeared in the
Newsletter of the Anthroposophical Society of America.
Permission to print them is gratefully acknowledged.

The translations were done for the most part by
Maria St.Goar from the original German.

They appear in German as lecture notes not revised by the
lecturer in: *Anthroposophie, soziale Dreigliederung und
Redekunst*, published by the Rudolf Steiner
Nachlassverwaltung, Dornach, Switzerland, 1971,
Bibliographie-Nr.339.

Cover Design by Peter van Oordt

ISBN 978-1-957569-39-0

MERCURY PRESS
an imprint of SteinerBooks
PO Box 58, Hudson, NY 12534
www.steinerbooks.org

Printed in the United States of America
by Integrated Books International

Contents

Introduction

Gisela O'Neil
editor of the *Newsletter of the Anthroposophical Society in America*

Lecturing is an art that requires command of many technical aspects. The novice tells all he knows, or worse – what he has read about a subject. He either bores or overwhelms the listeners with his flow of information. The master knows his audience and calls forth wonder and insight. How is it done?

In 1921, to provide prospective lecturers with some guidance, Rudolf Steiner gave two courses on the art of lecturing: one in Stuttgart and the one published here, in Dornach. The illustrative material needed in all lecturing was taken from the theme and purpose of these lectures: speaking on the need for a threefold social organism. The Swiss political and social situation at that time was relevant to the audience of about fifty Swiss members of the Anthroposophical Society.

These lectures were not intended for publication and were printed only fifty years later, in 1971. They were translated into English for the *Newsletter of the Anthroposophical Society* and serialized in nine issues, Autumn 1976 to Winter 1978.

Summer 1983.

Lecture 1

My intention in this course is to address the question: What is necessary for really supporting the movement of Anthroposophy and the threefold social order – insofar as this movement is of concern today? The course will therefore not be directed towards lecturers in general; it is meant to be a kind of orientation course for the personalities who have made it their task to work in the direction indicated.

Personalities who receive what can come from Anthroposophy simply as a kind of information will not get much from this course. Indeed, at present, we definitely need activity within our movement. It seems to be difficult to kindle this activity. It seems difficult to spread the insight that this activity is really necessary in our time.

Hence, it will not be a matter of a formal course in lecturing, but rather, of just those things that are necessary for someone who would like to accomplish the quite definite task: The one just indicated.

On the whole, the anthroposophical movement has no use for general talk. Indeed, this is exactly the mark of our present culture and civilization that there is general talk about things. People do not pick up concrete tasks. They prefer to talk in general terms.

Hence, I do not intend to treat the things in this course that I shall discuss as regards content in such a way that they might serve as information. But I shall try to treat these things in such a way – and this must indeed be the case in such an orientation course because it is intended as the very basis for a definite task – in such a way that they can then link up directly with the spoken word. And I shall treat this spoken word in a way that takes into consideration that he who sets himself the task of delivering a lecture for Anthroposophy is perhaps not working under conditions in which interest is already present, but is working to awaken interest by the first few lectures. Thus, I should like to shape this course in this quite concrete sense.

And, even the large points of view that I shall discuss today are to be meant entirely in this quite concrete sense. One would be reporting what is incorrect if – as is so popular nowadays – one set down what I shall say both today and in the next days as abstract sentences.

Today I intend to speak of certain set rules.

Whenever, through a lecture, one sets out to bring something home to one's fellow man, a responsive interchange will naturally take place between the person who has something to communicate, something to work for, something to be enthusiastic about, and the persons who listen to him. An interplay of soul forces occurs. And to this interplay of soul forces we propose at first to turn our attention.

As you know, these soul forces live in thinking, feeling and willing. And a single soul force is never active in abstract form by itself. The other soul forces play into each soul force, so that when we think, feeling and willing are also always active in our thinking, as are thinking and willing in our feeling, and thinking and feeling in our willing.

But still, one cannot consider the soul life – both by itself and in its responsive interchange between people – except from the point of view of this tending on the one side to thinking, and on the other to willing. And so, in the sense of our task today, we must know the following:

What we think interests nobody else, and whoever believes that his thoughts – insofar as they are thoughts – interest any other person, will not be able to apply himself to the task of lecturing. (We intend to speak more precisely about these things.) The will to which we would like to fire a gathering, or even one other person, this will that we wish to put into our lecture, this annoys people, this they instinctively reject.

When one approaches people as a lecturer, then one has to do chiefly with the workings of various instincts: The thinking that one kindles in oneself does not interest people. Will annoys them. Thus, if some one were called upon for this or that act of will, we would find that we had called up, not his will, but his annoyance. And if we were to sketch our most beautiful and ingenious ideas in a monologue before people, they would walk out. That must be the fundamental guideline for the lecturer.

I do not say that this is so when we consider a general conversation among people, a gossip session or the like. For I am not speaking here about how these two are to be treated. Rather, I am speaking of what should fill our souls, of what should live in us as the proper impulse for lecturing, if the lecture is to have a purpose precisely in the direction I now mean. I am speaking of the guideline one needs to set oneself: Our thoughts do not interest an audience – our will annoys every audience.

Now, we must take a further matter into consideration: When someone lectures, the fact is that he lectures for the most part not only out of his own being, but out of all kinds of situations. For instance, he lectures on some affair that for weeks, perhaps, has been discussed by, or described to many of the people who will be listening to him. He then naturally meets with quite a different interest than he does if his first sentences touch on something that, until now, had not occupied his hearers in the slightest. When some one lectures here in the Goetheanum, it is naturally something quite different from what it is when one lectures at a hotel in Kalamazoo. I mean, even setting aside the fact that in the Goetheanum one is likely to lecture to people who have occupied themselves for some time with the material, have read or heard about it, whereas this is probably not the case in Kalamazoo. I mean the whole surroundings: The fact that one comes to a building such as the Goetheanum makes it possible to turn to the public in quite another manner than is possible when one lectures at a hotel in Kalamazoo. And so there are countless circumstances out of which one lectures that must always be considered.

This however, establishes the necessity, especially in our time, of taking one's lead somewhat from what should not be to what should be. Let us take an extreme case. A typical, average professor was supposed to give a lecture. At first he deals with his thoughts about the object, and, if he is a typical, average professor, he also deals with the conviction that these thoughts that he thinks, on the whole, are the very best in the world on the subject in question. Everything else has at first no interest for him. He writes these thoughts down. And of course, when he commits these thoughts to paper, then they become fixed. He then sticks this manuscript into his left side pocket, goes off, unconcerned as to whether it is to the Goetheanum or to the hotel in Kalamazoo, finds a lecturer's podium that is set up in a suitable way, at the right distance for his eyes, lays his manuscript on it, and reads. I am not saying that every one does it this way. But it is a frequent occurrence and a characteristic procedure in our time. And it points to the horror one can have towards lecturing today. It is the type of lecturing for which one should have the greatest aversion.

And since I have said that our thoughts interest nobody else, and our will annoys everybody, then it seems that it is the feelings upon which lecturing depends, – that an especially significant cultivation of feeling must be basic for lecturing. Hence it becomes of significance, of perhaps remote, yet fundamental significance, that we have acquired this proper aversion for the extreme type of lecture-reading just mentioned.

I once heard a lecture by the renowned Helmholtz at a rather large meeting that was certainly given in this manner: The manuscript was taken out of the left side pocket and read off. Afterwards a journalist came to me and said: "Why wasn't this lecture printed, a copy slipped into the hand of each one there? And then Helmholtz could have gone about and extended his hand to each one!" The latter would have been more valuable perhaps to the hearers, than the terrible experience of sitting on the hard chairs to which they were condemned in order to have read to them the manuscript, which required more time than it would have taken them to read it themselves. (Most of them would have needed a very long time indeed if they wanted to understand it, but listening for a short time didn't help them at all.)

One must by all means reflect on all these concrete things if one wishes to understand how the art of lecturing can, in all truth and honesty, be striven for.

At the Philosophers' Congress in Bologna the main lecture was delivered in the following way: It lay on each chair, three copies, one in each of three languages. One had first to pick them up in order to be able to sit down on the empty chair. And then the lecture was read aloud from the printed copy, requiring somewhat more than an hour. Through such procedure even the most beautiful lecture is no longer a lecture, for understanding gained through reading is something essentially different from the understanding gained through listening. And these things must be considered if one wants to familiarize oneself in a vivid way with such tasks.

Certainly, even a novel can so move us that we shed tears at definite passages. I mean of course, that a good novel can do this only at definite passages, not from the beginning to the end. But what then is really present during reading so that we are carried away by what we read? Whenever we are carried away by what we read, we have to accomplish a certain work that coincides, that is connected very strongly, with the inner side of our humanity. This inner work that we accomplish when we read consists in this, that while we turn our glance to the single letters, we actually carry out what we have learned in the putting together of the letters. Through this activity of looking at the letters, putting them together and thinking about them, we draw forth a meaning. That is a process of receiving which occurs in our ether body and yet strongly engages the physical body in the perceiving.

But all this simply falls away when only listening. This whole activity does not occur when simply listening. Nevertheless, this listening activity is bound up in a definite way with the grasping of a thing. The person is in need of this activity whenever he wishes to grasp a thing.

He needs the cooperation of his ether body and in part, even of his physical body. Not only of the sense organ of the ear! Moreover, when listening, he needs a soul life so active that it is not exhausted in the astral body, but brings the ether body to pulsation, and then this ether body also brings the physical body to swing along with it.

What must take place as activity during reading must also be developed while listening to a lecture, but – I should like to say –

in quite another form when listening, because that activity cannot be there in the same way it is for reading. What is called up in reading is transformed feeling, feeling that has been pressed into the ether body and the physical body. This feeling becomes a force. As lecturers we must be in a position to bring up feeling as feeling content, even in the most abstract of lectures.

It is really a fact that our thoughts as such do not interest people, our will impulses annoy everybody, and only our feelings determine the impression, the effect – in a justified sense, of course – of a lecture.

Hence, there arises the most important question. How shall we be able to have something in our lecture that in a sufficiently strong way will enable the listener to bring forth the needed shade of feeling, the needed permeation with feeling – and yet not press him, lest we hypnotize or suggest.

There cannot be abstract rules by which one learns how to speak with feeling. For, in the person who has hunted in all sorts of manuals for the rules for speaking with feeling, one will notice that his lecturing most surely does not come from his heart, that it stems from quite another place than his heart. And truly, all lectures should come from the heart. Even the most abstract lecture should come from the heart. And that it can! And it is precisely this that we must discuss, how even the most abstract lecture can come from the heart.

We must understand quite clearly what is really stirring in the soul of the listener when he gives us his ear, not perhaps when we tell him something he is eager to hear, but when we expect him to want to listen to our words. Essentially it is indeed always a kind of attack on our fellow men when we fire a lecture at them. And that too is something of which we must be thoroughly aware, that it is an attack on the listeners, when we fire a lecture at them.

Everything I say – I must ever and again add parenthetically – is to be considered as a guide for the lecturer, not as a characteristic of social intercourse or the like. Were I to speak in reference to social intercourse, I could naturally not formulate the same sentences. They would be so much foolishness. For, when one speaks concretely, such a sentence as "Our thoughts interest no one" can be either something very clever or very stupid. Everything we say may be foolishness or good sense according to its whole human connection. It depends solely upon the way it is placed into the context. Hence, the lecturer needs quite other things than instructions in the formal art of lecturing.

Thus, it is a matter of recognizing what is really active in the listener. Sympathy and antipathy are active in the listener. These assert themselves more or less unconsciously when we attack the listener with a lecture. Sympathy or antipathy! For our thoughts however, he surely has no sympathy at first. Also not for our will impulses, for that which we, so to speak, want of him, for that to which we want to exhort him.

If we want somehow to approach the art of lecturing, we must have a certain understanding for the listener's sympathy and antipathy toward what we say. Sympathy and antipathy have in reality to do neither with thinking nor with the will, but operate here in the physical world exclusively for the feelings, for what has to do with feeling. A conscious awareness in the listener of sympathy and antipathy has the effect of obstructing the lecturer's approach to him – our awareness of sympathy and antipathy must be of such a kind that it never comes to the consciousness of the listener, especially during the lecture. Working to rouse sympathy and antipathy has the effect of making it seem that we fall over ourselves. Such, approximately, is the effect of a lecture when we want to arouse sympathy and antipathy.

We must have the finest understanding for sympathy and antipathy in the listener. During the lecture, however, his sympathy or antipathy should not concern us in the least. All that has an effect upon the sympathy and antipathy, if I may say so, we must bring into the lecture indirectly, beforehand, during the preparation.

Just as little as there can be instructions of an abstract kind for painting or sculptering, just so little can there be rules of an abstract kind for lecturing. But, just as one can stimulate the art of painting, so too it is possible to stimulate the art of lecturing.

And it is chiefly a matter of taking in full earnestness the things that can be pointed out in this direction.

In order to start from an example, let us first take the teacher speaking to children. As far as his speaking is concerned, actually the very least depends upon his genius and wisdom. As to whether we can teach mathematics or geography well, the very, very least will depend upon whether we ourselves are good mathematicians, or good geographers. We can be outstanding geographers, but poor teachers of geography. The intrinsic worth of the teacher, which surely rests in large measure upon his speaking, depends upon what he has previously felt and experienced about the things to be presented, and the kinds of feelings that are again stirred up by the fact that he has a child before him.

Thus it is, for example, that Waldorf School pedagogy amounts to knowledge of man, that is of the child – not to a knowledge of the child resulting from abstract psychology, but one that rests upon a fully human comprehension of the child. So far does this comprehension go that through feeling intensified to loving devotion, the teacher manages to experience with the child. Then there results – from this experiencing with the child and from what one has previously felt and experienced in the field in which one has to express something – from all this, there results quite instinctively the manner in which one has to speak and handle the class.

It doesn't serve at all, for instance, in instructing a slow child, to use the wisdom of the world that one has. Wisdom helps one in the case of a dull child, if one acquired the wisdom yesterday and used it in one's preparation. At the moment of instruction of the dull child, one must have the genius to be as slow as the child himself, and just have the presence of mind to remember the way in which one was wise yesterday, during the preparation. One must be able to be slow with the slow child, naughty, at least in feeling, with the naughty child, good with the good child, and so forth. As teacher one must be – I hope that this word will not arouse too great antipathy because it is directed too strongly towards thoughts or will impulses – one must really be a kind of chameleon, if one wishes to instruct rightly.

What many Waldorf teachers have, out of their genius, been able to do to increase discipline has pleased me very much. For example, a teacher is speaking about Jean Paul. The children start writing notes and passing them to each other. This teacher doesn't start reprimanding them; instead, he moves into the situation, and with great patience finds out what it's all about. He then dissolves the threatened disturbance with some instruction on postal affairs. That is more effective than any reminder. The note-writing stops. This result rests naturally upon a concrete grasping of the moment. But of course, one must have the presence of mind. One must know that sympathy and antipathy which one wishes to stir, sit more deeply in the human being than one is accustomed to think.

And so it is extraordinarily important, whenever the teacher has to deal with some chapter in class, that he first of all call up vividly into consciousness during the preparation how he himself approached this chapter when he was the same age as his children are, how he felt then – not in order to become pedantic, of course, not in order when he treats it on the next day to succeed in feeling again as he once did! No, it is enough when this feeling is brought up during the preparation, when it is experienced in the preparation, and then it is a matter of working on the very next day with the knowledge of man just described.

Thus, here also, in teaching, it is a question of finding within ourselves the possibility of shaping the lecture material that is part of one's teaching material, out of feeling.

We can best become aware of how these things can work if we also bring the following before our soul's eye: whenever something of a feeling character is to work into what pulses through our lecture, then naturally we may not speak thoughtlessly, although thoughts do not really interest our listeners, and we may not lecture without will, albeit our will annoys them. We shall very often even want to speak in such a way that what we say goes into the will impulses of the people, that in consequence of our lecture our fellowmen want to do something. But we must not under any circumstances so organize the lecture that we bore the listeners through our thought content and arouse their antipathy through the will impetus we seek to give.

So it is a matter of establishing the thinking for the lecture, completely establishing it, as long as possible before we lecture; that we have beforehand absolutely settled the thought element within ourselves. This has nothing to do with whether we then speak fluently, or whether we speak haltingly. The latter, as we shall see, depends upon quite other circumstances. But what must, to a degree, work unconsciously in the lecture, is connected with our having settled the thought content within ourselves much, much earlier. The thought monologue, which should be as lively as possible, we must have rehearsed earlier, letting it take form out of the arguments for and against, which we ourselves bring forward during this preparation, anticipating all objections as much as possible.

Through this manner of experiencing our lecture in thoughts beforehand, we take from it the sting it otherwise has for the audience. We are, to a degree, bound to sweeten our lecture by having gone through the sourness of the logical development of the train of thought beforehand – but, as much as possible in such a way that we do not formulate the lecture word for word. Of course, matters cannot be taken literally – namely, that we have no idea of how we shall formulate the sentences when we begin to lecture. But the thought content must be settled. To have the verbal formulation ready for the whole lecture is something that can never lead to a really good lecture. For that already comes very near to having written the lecture down, and we need but to imagine that a phonograph instead of us stood there and gave it out automatically. When the lecture is given word for word, from memory, then the difference between this and a machine that turns it out automatically is even smaller than it is between a lecture read from a manuscript and the machine that turns it out automatically. Moreover, if we have formulated a lecture beforehand, so that it is worked out in such a way that it can be spoken by us verbatim, then we are indeed not differentiating ourselves very strongly from a machine by which we have recorded the lecture and then let it be played back. There is not much difference between listening to a lecture that is spoken word for word as it was worked out and reading it oneself, – aside from the fact that in reading one is not continually disturbed by the lecturer, as one is continually when listening to him deliver a lecture that he has memorized.

The thought preparation is experienced in the correct manner when it is carried to the point at which the thoughts have become absolutely part of oneself, and this all well before the lecture. One must be finished with what one would present.

To be sure, there are some exceptions for ordinary lectures that one delivers to an audience until then unknown to one. Whenever, before such an audience, one begins immediately with what one has to a degree worked out meditatively in thoughts, and speaks from the first sentence on under direct inspiration, if I may say so, then one does not do something really good for the listeners. At the beginning of a lecture one must make one's personality somewhat active. At the beginning of a lecture one should not immediately entirely extinguish one's personality, because the vibration of feeling must first be stirred.

Now, it is not necessary to proceed as did, for example, Michael Bernays, Professor of History of German Literature, at one time very famous in certain circles. He once came to Weimar to give a lecture on Goethe's *Color Theory*, and wanted to form his first sentences in such a way that certainly the feeling of the listeners would be engaged very, very intensively – but, to be sure, it happened quite otherwise than he had intended. He arrived in Weimar several days before the lecture. Weimar is a small city where one can go about among people (some of whom will be in the hall) and make propaganda for one's lecture. Those who hear about the lecture directly tell others about it, and the whole hall is really "tuned up" when one delivers one's lecture. Now Prof Michael Bernays actually went about in Weimar for several days and said: "Oh, I have not been able to prepare myself for this lecture: my genius will surely prompt me correctly at the right moment." He was to deliver this lecture in the Recreation Hall in Weimar. It was a hot summer day. The windows had to be opened. And, directly in front of this Recreation Hall there was a poultry yard. Michael Bernays took his place and waited for his genius to begin suggesting something to him. For indeed, all Weimar knew that his genius must come and suggest his lecture to him. And then, at this moment, while Bernays was waiting for his genius, the cock outside began: cock-adoodle-doo! Now every one knew: Michael Bernays' genius has spoken for him! – Feelings were strongly stirred. To be sure, in a different way from what he wanted. But there was a certain atmosphere in the hall.

I do not recount this in order to tell you a neat anecdote, but because I must call your attention to the following: the body of a lecture must have been so formed that it is well worked through meditatively in thoughts, and later formulated freely, – but the introduction is really there for the purpose of making oneself a bit ridiculous. That inclines the listeners to listen to one more willingly. If one does not make oneself a wee bit ridiculous – to be sure, so that it's not too obvious, so that it flows down only into the unconscious – one is unable to hold the attention in the right way when delivering a single lecture. Of course, it should not be exaggerated, but it will surely work sufficiently in the unconscious.

What one should really have for every lecture is this – that one has verbally formulated the first, second, third, fourth, and at most, the fifth sentences. Then one proceeds to the development of the material that has been worked out in the way I have just indicated. And one should have verbally formulated the closing sentences. For, in winding up a lecture, if one is a genuine lecturer, one should really always have some stage fright, a secret anxiety that one will not find one's last sentence. This stage fright is necessary for the coloring of the lecture; one needs this in order to captivate the hearts of the listeners at the end: – that one is anxious about finding the last sentence. Now, if one is to meet this anxiety in the right way, after one has perspiringly completed one's lecture, let one add this to all the rest of the preparation, that one bear in mind the exact formulation of the last one, two, three, four – at most, five – sentences. Thus, a lecture should really have a frame: The formulation of the first and last sentences. And, in between, the lecture should be free. As mentioned, I give this as a guiding principle.

And now perhaps, many of you will say: yes, but if one is not able to lecture just that way? One need not therefore immediately say that it would be so difficult, that one should not lecture at all. It is indeed quite natural that one can lecture a bit better or a bit worse, just so long as one does not let oneself be deterred from lecturing because of all these requirements: but one should make an effort to fulfill these requirements, at the same time as one makes such guiding principles as we develop here pervade all that he strives to do.

And there is indeed a very good means for becoming at least a bearable lecturer, even if at first one is no lecturer, even the opposite of a lecturer. I can assure you that when the lecturer has made himself ridiculous fifty times, that his lecture will come out right the fifty-first time. Just because he made himself ridiculous fifty times. And he for whom fifty times do not suffice, can undertake to lecture a hundred times. For one day it comes right, if one does not shy away from public exposure. One's last lecture before dying will naturally never be good if one has previously shied away from public exposure. But, at least the last lecture before one's death will be good if one has previously made oneself ridiculous a certain number of times. This is also something about which one should really always think. And one will thus surely train oneself to be a lecturer! To be a lecturer requires only that people listen to one, and that one come not too close to them, so to speak, that one really avoid anything that comes too close to the people.

One's usual manner of speaking in social life when conversing with other people will not be fitting when delivering a lecture in public, or generally speaking, to an audience. At most, one will be able to insert sentences such as one speaks in ordinary life only now and then. It is well to be aware that what one has as formulation of one's speaking in ordinary life, is, as a rule, somewhat too subtle or too blunt for a lecture to an audience. It just does not sit quite right. The way one usually formulates one's words to another person varies; it always swings between being somewhat crude or, on the other hand, somewhat untruthful or impolite. Both must be entirely avoided in a lecture delivered to an audience, and, if used, then only in parenthesis, so to speak. Otherwise the listener has the secret feeling: while the lecturer begins to speak as one does in a lecture, suddenly he starts declaiming, or presenting a dialogue, – he must intend either to offend us a bit or to flatter us.

We must also bring the will element into the lecture in the right way. And this can only be accomplished by our preparation, but by such preparation as uses one's own enthusiasm in thinking through the material, enthusiasm that to a certain extent lives with the material.

Now consider the following: first one has completed the thought content, made it one's own. The next part of the preparation would be to listen, so to speak, to oneself inwardly lecturing on this thought content. One begins to listen attentively to these thoughts. They need not be formulated verbatim, as I have already said, but one begins to listen to them. It is this which puts the will element into the right position, this listening to oneself. For while we listen to ourselves inwardly, we develop enthusiasm or aversion, sympathy or antipathy at the right places, as these responses follow what we wish to impart. What we prepare in this willed way also goes into our will, and appears during our lecturing in tone variation. Whether we speak intensively or more softly, whether we accentuate brightly or darkly, this we do solely as the result of the feeling-through and willing-through of our thought content in the meditative preparation.

We must gradually lead all the thought content over into the forming of a picture of the composition of our lecture. Then the thinking will be embedded in the lecture, not in the words, but between the words, in the way the words, the sentences, and the arrangement are shaped. The more we are in a position to think about the *how* of our lecture, the more strongly we work into the will of the others. What people will accept depends upon what we put into the formulation, into the composition of the lecture.

Were we to come to them and say: "When all is said and done, every one of you who does not do his utmost in order to realize the threefold social order tomorrow is a bad fellow" – that would annoy people. However, when we present the sense of the threefold social order in a lecture that is composed in accordance with the nature of its content, that it is inwardly organized so that it is itself even a kind of intimate 'threefolding' and especially even if it is so fashioned that we ourselves are convinced of the necessity for the threefold social order, convinced with all our feeling and all our will impulses – then this works upon the people, works upon the will of the people.

What we have done in the way of developing our thoughts in order to make our lecture into a work of art, this affects the people's will. What springs from our own will, what we ourselves want, what fills us with enthusiasm, what enraptures us, this affects more the thinking of the listeners, this stimulates them more easily in their thoughts.

Thus it is that a lecturer who is enthusiastic about his subject is easily understood. A lecturer who composes artistically will more easily stir the will of his listeners. But the main principle, the chief guideline must still be this: That we deliver no lecture that is not well prepared.

Yes, but when we are compelled to deliver a lecture on the so-called spur of the moment; when, for example, we are challenged and have to answer immediately; then we certainly cannot turn back in time to the preceding day when we brought the argument to mind, in order to meditate on its counterargument – that cannot be done! And yet, it can be done! It can be done in just such a moment by being absolutely truthful. Or we are attacked by a person who accosts us in a terribly rude manner, so that we must answer him immediately. Here we have a strong feeling fact at the outset! Thus, the feeling is already stirred in a corresponding way. Here is a substitute for what we otherwise use in order to experience with enthusiasm what we first represent to ourselves in thought. But then, if we say nothing else in such a moment except what as a whole person can say at each moment when we are attacked in this manner, then we are nevertheless prepared in a similar way in this situation too.

Just in such things it is a question of the unwavering decision to be only, only, only truthful, and when the attack is not such that we are challenged to a discussion, then there are present, as a rule, all the conditions for understanding. (I shall speak about this later.) It is then actually a question not of delivering mere lectures, but of doing something quite different, which will be particularly important for us if we wish to complete this course rightly. For indeed, in order to be active in the sense that I indicated today at the beginning, we shall have not merely to deliver lectures, but every one of us will also have to stand his ground in the discussion period, come what may. And about this, much will have to be said, in fact, very much.

Now I beg you above all, to look at what I have said today from the point of view that it indicates perhaps a bit the difficulty of acquiring the art of lecturing. But it is quite especially difficult when it is necessary not only to lecture, but even to have to lecture about lecturing. Just think if one were to paint painting, and sculpture sculpturing!

Thus, the task is not altogether easy. But we shall nevertheless try in some way to complete it in the coming days.

Lecture 2

When we set out today to speak about Anthroposophy and the threefold movement with its various consequences – which indeed arise out of Anthroposophy, and must really be thought of as arising out of it, – then we must first of all hold before our souls that it is difficult to make oneself understood. And, without this feeling – that it is difficult to make oneself understood – we shall hardly be able to succeed as lecturers for anthroposophical spiritual science and all that is connected with it, in a way satisfying to ourselves. For if there is to be a way of speaking about Anthroposophy that is appropriate, then this speaking must be entirely different from what one is accustomed to in accordance with the traditions of speaking. One has often fallen into the habit of speaking also about anthroposophical matters in the way one has become used to speaking in the age of materialism; but one is more apt thereby to obstruct understanding for Anthroposophy than to open up an approach to it.

We shall first of all have to make quite clear to ourselves what the content of the matter is that comes towards us in Anthroposophy and its consequences. And as I said yesterday, I shall deal in these lectures with the practice of lecturing, but only for anthroposophical and related matters, so that what I have to say applies only to these.

We must now make clear to ourselves that it is primarily the feeling for the central issue of the threefold social order that must at first be stirred in our present humanity. It must after all be assumed that an audience of today does not begin to know what to do with the concept of the threefold social order. Our speaking must slowly lead to the imparting first of all of a feeling for this threefold social order in the audience.

During the time when materialism has held sway, one has become accustomed to giving expression to the things of the outer world through description. In this one had a kind of guidance in the outer world itself. Moreover, objects in the outer world, I would say, are too fixed for one to believe that it ultimately makes much difference how one speaks about them; one need only give people some guidance on how to perceive this outer world. Then, in the end it comes to this: if, let us say, one delivers somewhere a popular lecture with experiments, and thereby demonstrates to people how this or that substance reacts in a retort, then they see how the substance reacts in the retort. And whether one then lectures this way or that way – a bit better, a bit less well, a bit more relevantly, a bit less relevantly – in the end makes no difference. And gradually it has tended to come to the point that such lectures and such talks are attended in order to see the experimenting, and what is spoken is just taken along as a kind of more or less agreeable or disagreeable background noise. One must express these things somewhat radically, just in order to show the exact direction in which civilization is moving in regard to these things.

When it is a matter of what to stimulate in people for doing, for willing, one believes that one must just "set up ideals." People would have to accustom themselves to "apprehend ideals," and thus one gradually slips more and more over into the utopian element, when it is a matter of such things as the threefold ordering of the social organism.

So it has also often happened that many people who lecture about the threefold idea today absolutely call forth the opinion, through the manner in which they speak, that it is some utopia or other that should be striven for. And, since one is always of the opinion that what should be striven for in most cases cannot be expected to come in less than fifty or a hundred years – or many extend the time even further – so one also allows oneself, quite unconsciously, to approach speaking about things as if they would first ripen in fifty or a hundred years. One slips away from the reality very soon, and then talks about it thus: How will a small shop be set up in the threefold social organism? What will be the relation of the single person to the sewing machine in the threefold social organism? – and so on. Such questions are really put in abundance to any endeavor such as the threefolding of the social organism. As regards such an endeavor, which with all of its roots comes out of reality, one should not at all speak in this utopian fashion. For one should always evoke at least this feeling: the threefold ordering of the social organism is nothing that can be "made" in the sense that state constitutions can be made in a parliament – of the kind for example, that the Weimar National Assembly was. These are made! But one cannot speak in the same sense of making the threefold social organism.

Just as little can one speak of "organizing" in order to produce the threefold social order. What an organism *is*, this one does not organize; this grows. It is just in the nature of an organism that one does not have to organize it, that it organizes itself. That which can be organized is no organism. We must approach things from the start with these feelings; otherwise we will not find the appropriate expression.

The threefold social order is indeed something that simply follows from the natural living together of people. One can falsify this natural living together of people – as has been the case, for example, in recent history – by extending the characteristic features of one member, the rights sphere, to both others. Then these two other members will simply become corrupted, because they cannot prosper, just as someone cannot get on well in an unsuitable garment, that is too heavy, or the like.

It is in the natural relation of people that the threefold order of the social organism lives, that the independent spiritual life lives, that the rights life, regulated by the people's majority, lives, that the economic life, shaped solely out of itself, also lives. One can put strait jackets on the spiritual life, on the economic life, although one does not need them; but then its own life asserts itself continually nevertheless, and what we then experience outwardly is just this self-assertion. Hence it is necessary to show that the threefolding of the social organism is implicit in the very nature of both the human being and the social life.

We see that the spiritual life in Europe was entirely independent and free until the 13th or 14th centuries, when the free, independent spiritual life was pushed into the universities. At that time you find the founding of universities, which in turn slip by and by into the life of the state. So that one can say: From about the 13th to the 16th or 17th century, the universities slip into the rights life, into the life of the state, taking the other educational institutions along with them, without people really noticing it. These other institutions simply followed. This we have on the one hand.

On the other hand, until about the same period, we have free economic rule that found its true, middle-European expression in the free economic village communities. As the free spiritual life slipped into the universities, which are localized at first, and which later find shelter in the state, so does the economic organization first receive a certain administration in the "rights" sense, when the cities emerge more and more. Then the cities, in the first place, organize this economic life, while earlier, when the village communities were setting the pace, it had grown freely. And then we see how increasingly that which was centralized in the cities seeks protection in the larger territories of the states. Thus we see how the tendency of modern times ends in letting the spiritual life on the one hand, the economic life on the other, seek the protection of states that increasingly take on the character of domains constituted according to Roman law. This was actually the development in modern times.

We have reached that point in historical development where things can go no further like this, where a sense and a feeling for free spiritual life must once again be developed. When in a strait jacket, the spirit simply does not advance, because it only apparently advances, but in truth still remains behind; it can never celebrate real births, but at most renaissances. It is just the same with the economic life.

Today we simply stand in the age in which we must absolutely reverse the movement that has developed in the civilized world of Europe with its American annex. In our age, the opposite direction must set in. For what has gone on developing for a time must reach a point at which something new must set in. Otherwise one runs into the danger of doing as one would when, with a growing plant, one were to say that it should not be allowed to come to fruition, it should grow further, it should keep blooming on and on. Then it would grow thus: bring forth a flower; then no seed, but again a flower, again a flower, and so on. Therefore it is absolutely necessary to familiarize oneself inwardly with these things, and to develop a feeling for the historical turning point at which we stand today.

But, just as in an organism every detail is necessarily formed as it is, so everything in the world in which we live and which we help to shape, should be formed as it must be in its place in the sense of the whole. If you think realistically, you cannot imagine that your ear lobe could be formed at all differently from what it is, in conformity with your whole organism. Were your ear lobe only the least bit differently formed, then you would also have to have quite a different nose, different fingertips, and so forth. And just as the ear lobe is formed in harmony with the whole human being, so also the lecture in which something flows that is taking on new forms must be given in conformity with the whole.

Such a lecture cannot be delivered in the manner that one could perhaps learn from the sermon-lecture. For the sermon-lecture as we still have it today, rests on the tradition that really goes back to the old East, on a special attitude that the whole human being in the old East had toward speech. This characteristic was continued, so that it lived in a certain free way in Greece, lived in Rome, and shows its last spark most clearly in the particular relationship that the Frenchman has to his language. Not that I want to imply that every Frenchman preaches when he speaks; but a similar relationship, such as had to develop out of the Eastern relationship to language still continues to live on in a definite way in the French handling of speech, only entirely in a declining movement.

This element that we can observe here in regard to language came to expression when one still learned speaking from the professors, as one could later, but now in the declining phase – professors who really continued to live on as mummies of ancient times and bore the title "professor of elocution." In former times, at almost every university, in every school, also in seminaries and so on there was such a professor of elocution, of rhetoric. The renowned Curtius* of Berlin actually bore the title "professor of elocution" officially. But the whole affair became too dull for him, and he did not lecture on elocution, but only demonstrated himself as a professor of elocution through being sent out by the faculty council on ceremonial occasions, since that was always the task of the professor of elocution. Nevertheless, Curtius made it his business to discharge his duties at such ceremonial occasions by paying as little regard as possible to the ancient rules of eloquence. For the rest, it was too dull for him to be a professor of elocution in times in which professors of elocution did not fit anymore, and he lectured on art history, on the history of Greek art. But in the university catalog he was listed as "professor of elocution." This refers us back to an element that was present everywhere in speech in olden times.

Now, when we consider what is quite especially characteristic in the training of speech for the middle European languages, for German, for example, then indeed everything denoted in the original sense by the word "elocution" has not the least meaning. For, something flowed into these languages that is entirely different from what was peculiar to speaking in the times when elocution had to be taken seriously. In the Greek and Latin languages there is elocution. In the German language elocution is something quite impossible, when one looks inwardly at what is essential.

Today, however, we are living definitely in a time of transition. What was the speech element of the German language cannot continue to be used. Every attempt must be made to come out of this speech element and to come into a different speech element. This also is a task, in a certain sense, to be solved by anyone who wants to speak productively about Anthroposophy or the threefold idea. For only when a fairly large number of people are able to speak in this way, will Anthroposophy and the threefold idea be rightly understood in public, even in single lectures. Meanwhile, there are not a few who develop only a pseudo-understanding and pseudo-avowal for these.

---

* *Ernst Curtius*, 1814-1896, archeologist and historian.

If we look back on the special element in regard to speaking that was present in the times out of which the handling of elocution was preserved, we must say: It was then as if language grew out of the human being in quite a naive way, as his fingers grow, as his second teeth grow. Speaking and language, with its whole organization, resulted from the imitation process. And only after one had language did one come to the use of thinking.

And now it transpired that the human being, when speaking to others about any problem, had to see that the inner experience, the thought experience, to a certain extent clicked [*einschnappte]* into the language. The sentence structure was there. It was in a certain way elastic and flexible. And, more inward than the language was the thought element. One experienced the thought element as something more inward than the language, and let it click into the language, so that it fitted into it – just as one fits the idea of a statue or the like into marble. It was entirely an artistic treatment of the language. Even the way in which one was meant to speak in prose had something similar to the way in which one was to express oneself in poetry. Rhetoric and elocution had rules that were not at all unlike the rules of poetic expression. (So as not to be misunderstood, I should like to insert here that the development of language does not exclude poetry. What I now say, I say for older arts of expression, and I beg you not to interpret it as if I wanted to assert that there can be no more poetry at all today. We need but treat the language differently in poetry. But that does not belong here; I wanted to insert this only in parenthesis, so as not to be misunderstood.)

And when we now ask: How was one then supposed to speak in the time in which the thought and feeling content clicked into the language? One was supposed to speak beautifully! That was the first task: to speak beautifully. Hence, one can really only learn to speak beautifully today when one immerses oneself in the old way of speaking. There was beautiful speaking. And speaking beautifully is definitely a gift that comes to us from the East. It might be said: There, speaking beautifully arrived at the point that one really regarded singing, the singing of language, as the ideal of speaking. Preaching is only a form of beautiful speaking stripped of much of the beautiful speaking. For, completely beautiful speaking is ritualistic speaking. When ritualistic speaking pours itself into a sermon, then much is lost. But still, the sermon is a daughter of the beautiful speaking found in the ritual.

The second form that has come into evidence, especially in German and similar languages, is that in which it is no longer possible to distinguish properly between the word and the grasping of thought conveyed; the word has become abstract, so that it exempts itself, like a kind of thought. It is the element where the understanding for language itself is stripped off. It can no longer have something click into it, because one feels at the very outset that what is to be clicked in and the word vehicle into which something is to click are one.

For who is clear today, for example in German, when he writes down *Begriff* [concept], that this is the noun form of *begreifen* [to grasp; to comprehend]–*begreifen* (*greifen* with a prefix) is thus *das Greifen* an *etwas ausführen* [the carrying out of the grasping of something] – that *Begriff* is thus nothing other than the noun form for objective perceiving? The concept *Begriff* was formed at a time when there was still a living perception of the ether body, which grasps things. Therefore one could then truly form the concept of *Begriff*, because grasping with the physical body is merely an image of grasping with the ether body.

But, in order to hear *Begreifen* in the word *Begriff,* it is necessary to feel speech as an organism of one's own. In the element of speaking that I am now describing, language and concept always swim through one another. There is not at all that sharp separation which was once present in the East, where the language was an organism, was more external, and that which declared itself lived inwardly. What lived inwardly had to click into the linguistic form in speaking; that is, click in so that what lives inwardly is the content, and that into which it clicked was the outer form. And this clicking-in had to happen in the sense of the beautiful, so that one was thus a true speech artist when one wanted to speak.

This is no longer the case when, for example, one has no feeling any more for differentiating between *Gehen* [to go] and *Laufen* [to run] in relation to language as such. *Gehen*: two e's – one walks thither without straining oneself thereby; *e* is always the feeling expression for the slight participation one has in one's own activity. If there is an *au* in the word, this participation is enhanced. From running (*Laufen*) comes panting (*Schnaufen*) that has the same vowel sound in it. With this one's insides come into tumult. There must be a sound there that intimates this modification of the inner being. But all this is indeed no longer there today; language has become abstract. It is like our onward-flowing thoughts themselves, for the whole middle region, and especially also for the Western region of civilization.

It is possible to behold a picture, an imagination in every single word; and one can live in this picture as in something relatively objective. The person who faced language in earlier times considered it as something objective into which the subjective was poured. He would as little not have regarded it so, as he would have lost sight of the fact that his coat is something objective, and is not grown together with his body as another skin.

As against this, the second stage of language takes the whole organism of language as another soul skin, whereas formerly language was much more loosely there, I should like to say, like a garment. I am speaking now of the stage of language in which *speaking beautifully* is no longer taken into consideration first, but rather speaking correctly. In this it is not a question of rhetoric and elocution, but of logic. With this stage, which has come up slowly since Aristotle's time, grammar itself became logical to the point that the logical forms were simply developed out of the grammatical forms – one abstracted the logical from the grammatical. Here all has swum together: thought and word. The sentence is that out of which one evolves the judgment. But the judgment is in truth so laid into the sentence that one no longer experiences it as inherently independent. Correct speaking has become the criterion.

Furthermore, we see a new element in speaking arising, only used elsewhere at the wrong point – carried over to a quite wrong domain. Humanity owes beautiful speaking to the East. Correct speaking lies in the middle region of civilization. And we must look to the West when seeking the third element.

But in the West it arises first of all in a quite corrupted form. How does it arise? Well, in the first place, language has become abstract. The word organism is already almost thought organism. And this has gradually increased so much in the West, that there it would perhaps even be regarded as facetious to discuss such things. But, the third element does already exist there in a completely wrong domain.

You see, in America, just in the last third of the 19th century, a philosophical trend called "pragmatism" has appeared. In England it has been called "humanism." James is its representative in America, Schiller in England. Then there are personalities who have already gone about extending these things somewhat. The merit of extending this concept of humanism in a very beautiful sense is due to Professor MacKenzie who was here recently.

To what do these endeavors lead? – I mean now American pragmatism and English humanism. They arise from a complete skepticism about cognition: Truth is something that doesn't really exist! When we make two assertions, we actually make them fundamentally in order to have reference points in life. When one speaks about an "atom," one cannot provide any particular basis of truth for it; but it is useful to take the atomic theory as a foundation in chemistry; thus we set up the atom concept! It is serviceable; it is useful. There is no truth other than what lives in useful, life-serving concepts. "God," if he exists or not, this is not the question. "Truth," that is something or other which is of no concern to us. But it is hard to live pleasantly if one does not set up the concept of God; it is really good to live, if one lives as if there were a God. So, let us set it up, because it's a serviceable, useful concept for life. Whether the Earth began according to the Kant-Laplace theory and will end according to the mechanical warmth theory, from the standpoint of truth, no human being knows anything about this – I am now just simply reporting – but it is useful for our thinking to represent the beginning and end of the Earth in this way.

This is the pragmatic teaching of James, and also in essence, the humanistic teaching of Schiller. Finally, it is also not known at all whether the human being now, proceeding from the standpoint of truth, really has a soul. That could be discussed to the end of the world, whether there is a soul or not, but it is useful to assume a soul if one wants to comprehend all that the human being carries out in life.

Of course, everything that appears today in our civilization in one place spreads to other places. For such things that arose instinctively in the West, the German had to find something more conceptual, that permits of being more easily seen through conceptually; and from this the "As If" philosophy originated: whether there is an atom or not is not the question; we consider the phenomena in such a way "as if" there were an atom. Whether the good can realize itself or not, cannot be decided; we consider life in such a way "as if" the good could realize itself. One could indeed quarrel to the end of the world about whether or not there is a God; but we consider life in such a way that we act "as if" there were a God. There you have the "As If" philosophy.

One pays little attention to these things because one imagines: there in America sits James with his pupils; there in England sits Schiller with his pupils; there is Vaihinger, who wrote the "As If" philosophy: there are a few owls who live in a kind of cloud castle, and of what concern is it to other people!

Whoever has the ear for it, however, already hears the "As If" philosophy sounding everywhere today. Almost all human beings talk in the sense of the "As If" philosophy. The philosophers are only quite funny fellows. They always blab out what other people do unconsciously. If one is sufficiently unprejudiced for it, then one only seldom hears a human being today who still uses his words differently, in connection with his heart and with his whole soul, with his whole human being, who speaks differently than as though the matter were as he expresses it. One only does not usually have the ear to hear within the sound and tone color of the speaking that this "As If" lives in it, that fundamentally people over the whole of civilization are seized by this "As If."

Whereas things usually come to be corrupted at the end, here something shows itself to be corrupted at the beginning, something that in a higher sense must be developed for handling of speech in Anthroposophy, in the threefold social order and so on. These things are so earnest, so important, that we really should speak specially about them. For it will be a question of elevating the triviality, "We need concepts because they are useful for life," this triviality of a materialistic, utilitarian theory, of raising it up to the ethical, and perhaps through the ethical to the religious. For, if we want to work in the sense of Anthroposophy and the threefold social order, we have before us the task of learning *good speaking*, in addition to the beautiful speaking and the correct speaking that we can acquire from history. We must maintain an ear for good speaking.

Until now, I have seen little sign that it has been noticed, when, in the course of my lectures I have called attention to this good speaking – I have done it very frequently. In referring to this good speaking, I have always said that it is not only a question today that what is said be correct in the logical, abstract sense, but it is a matter of saying something in a certain connection or omitting it, not saying it in this connection. It is a question of developing a feeling that something should not only be correct, but that it is justified within its connection – that it can be either good in a certain connection or bad in a certain connection. Beyond rhetoric, beyond logic, we must learn a true ethics of speaking. We must know how we may allow ourselves things in a certain connection that would not at all be permitted in another connection.

Here I may now use an example close at hand, which could perhaps have already struck some of you who were present lately at the lectures: I spoke in a certain connection of the fact that, in reality, Goethe was not born at all. I said that for a long time Goethe endeavored to express himself through painting, through drawing, but that nothing came about from it. It then flowed over into his poetic works, and then again in the poetic works, as for example *Iphigenia*, or especially in *Natürliche Tochter* [*"Daughters of Nature*"], we have indeed poetic works that are not at all in the sentimental mode. People called these poems of Goethe's "marble smooth and marble cold," because they are almost sculptural, because they are three-dimensional. Goethe had genuine capacities that really did not become human at all; he was actually not born. – You see, in that connection in which I spoke lately, one could quite certainly say it. But imagine if someone were to represent it as a thesis in itself in the absolute sense! It would not only be illogical, it would of course be quite crazy.

To speak out of an awareness of a life connection is something different from finding the adequate or correct use of a word association for the thought and feeling involved. To let a pronouncement or the like arise at a particular place out of a living relationship, that is what leads over from beauty, from correctness, to the ethos of language – at which one feels, when a sentence is uttered, whether one may or may not say it in the whole context. But now, there is again an inward growing together, not with language, but with speaking. This is what I should like to call good speaking or bad speaking, aside from correct or incorrect speaking, comes good or bad speaking, in the sense in which I have just presented it.

Today the view is still widespread that there can be sentences that one forms and that can then be spoken on any occasion, because they have absolute validity. In reality, for our life in the present, there are no longer such sentences. Every sentence that is possible in a certain connection is impossible today in another connection. That means, we have entered upon an epoch of humanity's development in which we need to direct our view to this many-sidedness of living situations.

The Eastern person who with his whole thinking lived within a small territory, also the Greek still, who with his spiritual life, with his rights life, with his economic life, lived in a small territory, poured something into his language that appears as a linguistic work of art must appear. How is it though in a work of art? It is such that a single finite object really appears infinite in a certain realm. In this way beauty was even defined, though one-sidedly, by Haeckel, Darwin and others: It is the appearance of the idea in a self-contained picture. – The first thing that I had to oppose in my Vienna lecture on "Goethe as the Father of a New Aesthetics," was that the beautiful is "the appearance of the idea in outer form." I showed then that one must mean just the reverse: that the beautiful arises when one gives to form the appearance of the infinite.

And so it is with language, which in a certain way also acts as a limited territory – as a territory that encloses the possible meaning within boundaries. If that which is actually infinite in the inner soul- and spirit life is to click into this language, it must there come to expression in beautiful form.

In correct speaking the language must be adequate; the sentence must fit the judgment, the concept, the word. The Romans were compelled to this, especially as their territory became ever larger and larger; their language transformed itself from the beautiful into the logical. Hence the custom has been retained, of conveying logic to people precisely in the Latin language. (You have indeed learned logic quite well by it.)

But we are now once again beyond this stage. Now, it is necessary that we learn to experience language with ethos – that, to a certain extent, we gain a kind of morality of speaking in our lecturing, while we know that we have in a certain context to allow ourselves something or to deny ourselves something. There, things do not click in, in the way I described earlier, but here we make use of the word to characterize. All defining ceases; here we use the word to characterize. The word is handled in such a way that one really feels each word as something insufficient, every sentence as something insufficient, that one has the urge to characterize that which one wishes to place before humanity from the most varied aspects – to go around the matter to a certain extent, and to characterize it from the most varied aspects.

I have often emphasized that this must be Anthroposophy's manner of presenting things. I have often emphasized that one should not indeed believe that one is able to find the adequate word do, the adequate sentence; one can only conduct oneself as a photographer does who, in order to show a tree, takes at least four views.

Thus a conception that lives itself out in an abstract trivial philosophy such as pragmatism or humanism, must be raised up into the realm of the ethical. And then it must live first of all in the ethos of language. We must learn good speaking. That means that we must experience as regards speaking something of all that we otherwise experience in relation to ethics, to moral philosophy.

After all, the matter has become quite clear in modern times. In the speaking of theosophists we have an archaism simply conditioned through the language – archaic, namely as regards the materialistic coloration of the last centuries: "physical body" – well, it is thick; "ether body" – it is thinner, more nebulous; "astral body" – once again thinner, but still only thinner; 'I' – still thinner. Now, new members of the human being keep on coming up: they become even thinner. At last one no longer knows at all how one can reach this thinness, but in any case, it only becomes ever thinner and thinner. One does not escape materialism. This is indeed also the hallmark of this theosophical literature. And it is always the hallmark that appears, when these things are to be spoken about, from theoretical speaking, to that which I once experienced within the Theosophical Society in Paris, (I believe it was in 1906). A lady there who was a real rock-solid theosophist, wanted to express how well she liked particular lectures that had been given in the hall in which we were; and she said: "There are such good vibrations here!" And one perceived from her that this was really thought of as something that one might sniff. Thus, the scents of the lectures that were left behind and that one could sniff out somehow, these were really meant.

We must learn to tear language away from adequacy. For it can be adequate only for the material. If we wish to use it for the spiritual, in the sense of the present epoch of development of humanity, then we must free it. Freedom must then come into the handling of language. If one does not take these things abstractly, but livingly, then the first thing into which the philosophy of freedom [spiritual activity] must come is in speaking, in the handling of language. For this is necessary; otherwise the transition will not be found, for example, to the characterization of the free spiritual life.

You see, for free spiritual life – that is to say spiritual life that exists out of its own laws – there is as yet not very much understanding in present-day humanity. For, mostly what is understood by free spiritual life is a structure in which people live, where each one crows his own cock-a-doodle-doo from his own dung heap – please excuse the picture – and in which the most incredible consonances come about from the crowing. In reality, in free spiritual life, harmony comes about through and through, because the spirit, not the single egoists, lives – because the spirit can really lead its own life over and above the single egoists.

For example there is definitely a Waldorf School spirit present in our Waldorf School in Stuttgart that is independent of the body of teachers, a spirit into which the body of teachers grows, and in which it becomes more and more clear that possibly a teacher can be more capable or less capable, but the spirit has a life of its own.

It is an abstraction when people speak today of "free spirit." This is no reality at all. The free spirit is something that really lives among people; one must only let it come into existence; one must only let what works among people come into existence.

What I have said to you today I have also said only so that what we are meant to gain here may proceed from fundamental feelings, from the feeling for the earnestness of the matter. I cannot, of course, suppose that every one will now go right out and, as those in olden times spoke beautifully, in the middle period correctly, now all will speak well! But you may not for this reason object: Of what help, then, are all our lectures, if we are not at once able to speak in the sense of good speaking? It is rather a matter of our really acquiring a feeling for the earnestness of the situation that we are thus to live into, so that we know: What is wanted here is something in itself so organically whole, that a necessity of form must gradually express itself even in speech, just as a necessity of form expresses itself in the ear lobe, which must be in harmony with the whole human being.

Thus I shall try to bring still closer together what is for us the content of Anthroposophy and the threefold social order with the way in which it should be presented to people. And, from the consideration of principles I shall come more and more into concreteness, and to that which should underlie the practice of lecturing.

Lecture 3

Along with the tasks that one can set oneself in a certain realm as a speaker it will be a question at first of entering in the appropriate way into the material itself that is to be dealt with. There are two ways of entering into the material, insofar as the message about this material is concerned in speaking. The first is to convert to one's own use the material for a lecture so that it can be divided up so that one is placed in the position of giving a composition to the lecture. Without composition a talk cannot really be understood. This or that may appeal to the listener about a lecture that is not composed; but in reality a non-composed lecture will not be assimilated. As far as the preparation is concerned, it must therefore be a matter of realizing: that every talk will inevitably be poor as regards its reception by the listeners that has merely originated in one's conceiving one statement after the other, one sentence after the other, and going through them to a certain extent, one after the other, in the preparation. If one is not in the position, at least at some stage of the preparation, of surveying the whole lecture as a totality, then one cannot really count on being understood. Allowing the whole lecture to spring, as it were, from a comprehensive thought, which one subdivides, and letting the composition arise by starting out from such a comprehensive thought comprising the total lecture, – this is the first consideration.

The other is the consulting of all the experiences that one has available out of immediate life for the subject of the lecture, that is, calling to mind as much as possible everything one has experienced first-hand about the matter in question; and, after one has before one a kind of composition of the lecture, one en-deavors to let the experiences flow here or there into this composition.

In general, that will be the rough draft in preparing. Thus, during one's preparation, one has the whole of the lecture before one as in a tableau. One has this tableau so exactly before one, that, as will indeed naturally be the case, one can incorporate the single experiences one remembers in the desired way here or there, as though one had written on paper: a, b, c, d. There is now an experience one knows belongs under d, another under f, another belongs under a, – so that one is to a certain extent independent of the sequence of the thoughts as they are afterwards to be presented, as regards this collecting of the experiences. Whether such a thing is done by putting it onto paper, or whether it is done by a free process without having recourse to the paper, will determine only that he who is dependent upon the paper will speak worse, and he who is not dependent upon the paper will speak somewhat better. But one can of course by all means do both.

But now it is a matter of fulfilling a third requirement, which is: after one has the whole on the one hand – I never say the 'skeleton' – and on the other hand the single experiences, one has need of elaborating the ideas that ensue to the point that these things can stand before the soul in the most complete inner satisfaction.

Let us take as an example, that we want to hold a lecture on the threefold social order. Here we shall say to ourselves: After an introduction – we shall speak further about this – and before a conclusion – about which we shall also speak – the composition of such a lecture is really given through the subject itself. The unifying thought is given through the subject itself. I say that for this example. If one lives properly, mentally, then this is valid actually for every single case; it is valid equally for everything. But let us take this example near at hand of the threefolding of the social organism, about which we want to speak. There, at the outset, is given that which yields us three members in the treatment of our theme. We shall have to deal with the nature of the spiritual life, the nature of the juridical-state life, and the nature of the economic life.

Then it will certainly be a question of our calling forth in the listeners, by means of a suitable introduction – about which, as mentioned, we shall speak further – a feeling that it makes sense to speak about these things at all, about a change in these things, in the present. But then it will be a matter of not immediately starting out with explanations of what is to be understood by a free spiritual life, by a juridical-states life founded on equality, by an economic life founded on associations, but rather of having to lead up to these things. And here one will have to lead up through connecting to that which is to hand in the greatest measure as regards the three members of the social organism in the present – what can therefore be observed the most intensively by people of today. Indeed, only by this means will one connect with what is known.

Let us suppose we have an audience, and an audience will be most agreeable and sympathetic that is a mixture of middle class people, working-class people – in turn with all possible nuances – and, if there are then of course also a few of the nobility – even Swiss nobility – it doesn't hurt at all. Let us therefore assume we have such a varied audience, made up of all social classes. I stress this because as a lecturer one should really always sense to whom one has to speak, before one sets about speaking. One ought already to transpose oneself actively into the situation in this way.

Now, what will one have to say to oneself to begin with about that which one can connect with in a present-day audience, as regards the threefold social organism? One will say to oneself: it is extraordinarily difficult in the first place to connect onto concepts of an audience of the bourgeois, because in recent times the bourgeoisie have formed extraordinarily few concepts about social relationships, since they have vegetated thoughtlessly to some extent as regards the social life. It would always make an academic impression, if one wanted to speak about these things today out of the circle of ideas of a middle-class audience. On the other hand, however, one can be clear about the fact that exceptionally distinct concepts exist concerning all three domains of the social organism within the working-class population – also distinct feelings, and a distinct social volition. And it means that it is nothing short of the sign of our present time, that precisely within the proletariat these qualified concepts are there.

These concepts are to be handled by us, though, with great caution, since we shall very easily call forth the prejudice that we want to be partisan in the proletarian direction. We should really combat this prejudice through our whole bearing. We shall indeed see that we immediately arouse for ourselves serious misunderstandings if we proceed from proletarian concepts. These misunderstandings have revealed themselves in point of fact constantly in the time when an effect could still be brought about in middle Europe, from about April 1919 on, for the threefolding of the social organism. A middle-class population hears only what it has sensed for decades from the fomenting behavior of the working class, out of certain concepts. How one views the matter oneself is then hardly comprehended at all.

One must be clear that being active in the world at all must be understood according to the way the world order works. The world order is such – you have only to look at the fish in the sea – that very, very many fish eggs are laid, and only a few become fish. That has to be so. But you must also reckon with this fact as you approach the tasks that are to be solved by you as speakers. Even if only very few people to begin with attend the first lecture and are but little moved by it, then actually one has attained the maximum of what can be attained. With things that one stands for in life, like the threefolding of the social organism, what can be accomplished by means of lecturing must never be abandoned, but must be taken up and perfected in some way, either through further lectures, or in some other way. It can be said: No lecture is really in vain that is given in this sense and to which is joined all that is required.

But one has to be absolutely clear about the fact that one will actually also be completely misunderstood by the proletarian population, if one speaks directly out of what they think today in accordance with their theories, as these have persisted for decades. One cannot ask oneself the question for instance: How does one do it so as not to be misunderstood? – One must only do it right! But for this reason it cannot be a matter of putting forward the question: Then how does one do it so as not to be misunderstood? That is easy to explain. One tells people what they have already thought anyway! One preaches to them, in some way, Marxism, or some such thing. Then one will of course be understood.

But there is nothing of interest in being understood in this way. For, one will indeed very soon have the following experience – concerning this experience one must be quite clear – : if one speaks today to a proletarian gathering so that they can at least understand the terminology – and that must be striven for – one will notice particularly in the discussion, that those who discuss have understood nothing. One usually doesn't get to know the others, since they do not participate in the discussions. Those who have understood nothing usually participate after such lectures in the discussions. And with them one will notice something along the following lines. (I have given countless lectures myself on the threefolding of the social organism to, as they are called in Germany, "surplus-value social democrats," independent "social democrats," communists and so on.) Now, one will notice that if someone enters the discussions and believes himself able to speak, then he usually answers one as though one had really not spoken at all, but as though someone or other had spoken more or less as one would have spoken as a social-democratic agitator thirty years ago in popular meetings. One feels oneself suddenly quite transformed. One says to oneself roughly the following: Well, can it then be that the misfortune has befallen you, that you were possessed in this moment by old Bebel?* That is really how you are confronted! Even physically the persons concerned hear nothing other than what they have been used to hearing for decades. Even physically – not merely with the soul – even physically they hear nothing other than what they have long been used to. And then they say: Well, the lecturer really told us nothing new! Because one was obliged to use the terminology, they have translated the whole connection of the terminology right away in the ear – not first in the soul – into that which they have been used to for a long time. And then

---

* *August Bebel*, 1840-1913. Founder in 1869 with *Wilhelm Liebknecht* of the Social-Democratic Party.

they talk on and on in the sense of what they have been used to for a long time.

This is the approximate course of countless discussions. At most, a new nuance entered into the matter when, from their newly attained standpoint, the Communists made an appearance and declared something like this: Above all else it is necessary to gain political power! Certainly, it is quite natural – I speak from experience and cite examples that actually occurred – that one first has to have political power. For instance, one person believed that if he had the political power of a head of the police, he would certainly not install himself as a registrar, since by profession he was a shoe repairman, and he could well understand that a shoe repairman could not know anything of the responsibilities of a registrar. Therefore, if he were head of the police (over the whole country), he would not make himself a registrar since he was only a shoe repairman! He did not realize that by saying this he really implied that while he felt quite well suited to be installed as Minister of the police, he did not consider himself qualified to be a registrar! This was a kind of new nuance for the discussion. The nuances were always approximately in this form.

Well, nevertheless, we must understand that in order to be comprehensible one must speak out of the inmost thoughts of the people. For, if one does that, their unconscious mind can follow somehow. This is particularly the case when the lecture is structured in the manner I have already indicated and shall elaborate on still further. But concerning the points that are really important, we must avail ourselves of concepts based on experience which, in this case, are concepts that can be formulated out of the experiences of the feelings of the working class.

Consider the spiritual part of the threefold social organism. Since the dawn of Marxism, the workman has developed quite definite concepts in regard to this spiritual aspect, namely the concept of ideology. He says: The spiritual life has no reality of its own. Religion, concepts of justice, concepts of morality, and so forth, art, science itself – these are nothing on their own. Only economic processes exist on their own. In world-historical development, one can follow how actual reality consists of how one level of the population relates to the other in economic life. From this factor of how one class relates to another in the life of the economy, the concepts, the feelings in religion, science, art, morals, rights, and so on, must evolve quite by themselves like a form of smoke that arises from something. So, rights, morality, religion, art are not realities but ideologies. In all social-democratic and other proletarian meetings, this expression, "ideology," along with the underlying sentiment that I have just characterized, could be heard for decades. It was nothing short of an especially developed means of indoctrination to make people understand that the middle class speaks of truth *per se*. It speaks of the values of morality and art, but all this has no standing in reality on its own; these are chimeras that arise from the economic process. One of the leaders of the working class, Franz Mehring,* carried this matter to special extremes in a book, *The Lessing Legend*.

A not very significant book by a typical middle-class professor, Erich Schmidt,† was published concerning Lessing. The reason why it isn't very significant is that it is not really Lessing who is being dealt with there, but a papier-mâché figure, wrongly designated as "Lessing," to which Erich Schmidt links the remarks, narrations and observations that he was capable of due to his special talent or lack of talent.

The reader is not dealing with a person at all in this book but with a made-up statue calling "Lessing." Before the book *Lessing* by Erich Schmidt had even been written, when I heard Erich Schmidt give a lecture in Vienna in the Academy of Sciences, where he presented the first beginnings of the first chapter of this book on Lessing in condensed form. I already knew that this middle-class professor did not have particularly clear conceptions about the living man Lessing but only a papier-mâché Lessing. At that time, I was strangely impressed by this speech, which demonstrated so clearly that if a person otherwise enjoys

---

* *Franz Mehring*, 1846-1919; socialist writer and politician, founder of Marxist literary analysis.

† *Erich Schmidt*, 1853-1913; literary historian.

a certain social standing and is allowed to speak, even in such a venerable academy of sciences, he need not say anything of real substance. For, at the most important points, where Erich Schmidt brought out something that was supposed to be characteristic of the personality whom he was discussing, he always said – singling out something of Lessing's manner of working or style of writing – "That's typical Lessing!" And this expression, "That's typical Lessing!" one heard, I believe, fifty times during this lecture at the academy.

Well, if one is dealing with John Smith from New Middletown, and one has to characterize him, relating the special way that he keeps up his compost heap, one will be able to say along the same lines, "That's typically Smith!" One will have made an equally weighty statement.

What I am saying is that we are dealing with something extraordinarily insignificant. But a proper social-democratic writer, as was Franz Mehring, ascribed the insignificance of Erich Schmidt's book on Lessing to the fact that Erich Schmidt was a middle-class professor, and so he said, "Well, that's a product of the bourgeoisie." And now he pitted his proletarian product against it, and he called his book *The Lessing Legend*. This book examines the economic conditions under which Lessing's forefathers had lived and what they did, how Lessing himself was placed in his youth within the life of the economy, how he had to become a journalist, how he had to borrow money – this is, after all, also an economical aspect – and so on. In short, it is shown how Lessing's conception of *Laocoon*, how his *Dramaturgy of Hamburg*, how his *Minna von Barnhelm* had to be the way they were because Lessing had grown out of certain economic conditions.

After the pattern of this book, *The Lessing Legend*, by the party-scholar Mehring, one of the students of my Worker's Education School – for many years, I taught in such an institution, even giving instruction in lecturing – proved in a trial speech that the Kantian philosophy originated simply from the economic conditions out of which Kant had developed. One always encountered matter similar to this in these circles and probably could find them still today, although by now they have more or less become empty phrases. But it was indeed so, and it meant that the modern member of the working class held the view that everything pertaining to the spiritual life is ideology.

With regard to the political life of rights, the proletarian only gives credence to what is once again established within economic conditions as relationships between people. For him, these are the social classes. The class holding power rules over the other classes. And a person belonging to a certain class develops class consciousness. Therefore, what the modern workman comprehends of the political life of rights is the class and what is close to his heart is class consciousness.

The third member of the social organism is the economic part. There too, clearly defined concepts exist within the working class, and the central concept that is referred to again and again, in the same manner as the concepts, ideology and class consciousness, is the concept of surplus value. The workman understands that when something is being produced, a certain value is attached to the economic product. Of this value, he receives a portion as compensation. The remainder is taken away for something else. He designates the latter as "surplus value," and occupies himself with this increment value, of which he has the feeling that he is deprived of it insofar as the value of the fruits of his labors are concerned.

Thinking these matters through in this manner, one can see how within that segment of the populace that has developed in recent times as the active and truly aggressive one, clearly defined concepts do in fact exist for the three spheres of the threefold social organism. The social life reveals itself in a threefold way – this is approximately how a proper proletarian theorist would put it – it reveals itself in the first place through its reality, through the value-producing economy. This value-producing economy does itself produce the surplus value out of the economic life. Through the balance of power that develops, socially active people are split into classes in the economic life, which represents the only reality; therefore, if they contemplate their human worth, they arrive at class consciousness, not human consciousness. And then there develops what one likes to have on Sundays, and what one needs – but also sort of inbetween – to properly invent machines, so that every so often, in one's free time, inventions can be made and so on; thus, ideology develops, which, however, results as a nebulous product out of the actual reality, out of the economic life.

I am really not drawing caricatures. I am only describing what dwelled in millions, not thousands, but millions of heads in the decades preceding the war, continuing also through the war. The working class therefore does have a concept of the threefoldness of the social organism, and one can relate to that.

One can relate to it in a still further sense. One can refer to the fact that in recent times the economic life has basically developed in a separate direction, since it contains its own inherent laws of necessity, and that the other elements of life, the spiritual life and the political life of rights, have lagged behind. People could not remain behind in the economic life. In the last third of the nineteenth century, they first had to change over to universal communications, then to the world economy. An inner necessity underlies that. In a certain sense, it develops by itself unless people ruin matters as was the case because of the war. But because other matters did not keep up the pace and because abstract intellectualism developed in them, awareness of the economic life became influential to an extraordinary degree and mainly affected people everywhere suggestively by its very nature. And this suggestive influence did not only take root in human conceptions but it turned into establishments. Intellectualism gradually has taken complete hold of the social life.

Abstraction, the abstract element, is the property of intellectualism. In life, one finds butter, let's say, or a Madonna by Raffael. Or one has a toothbrush or a philosophical work. In life, there are powder boxes for women, and so on. Life is made up of a lot of things, as you know. I could continue with this list endlessly. But you will not deny that these items differ very greatly from each other and that if one wants to gain concepts of all these things, these concepts will be very different from each other. But in the social life of recent times something developed nevertheless that became extremely significant for all relationships in life and that is not so very differentiated after all. For, we can say that a certain amount of butter costs two francs. A Madonna by Raffael costs two-million francs. A toothbrush costs only about two-and-a-half francs now. A philosophical work – which might be the least expensive – costs, shall we say, if it is a thin single volume, seventy rappen. A powder box, if it is of especially high quality, costs ten francs.

Now we've found a common denominator for the whole thing! Now we only need to consider the differences of the numbers, something that is part of one area. But we have spread an abstraction, the monetary value, over everything.

This has ingrained itself especially deeply into people's manner of thinking, although people do not always admit to it. Certainly, a person who is a poet considers himself as the world's most important point. He will therefore not evaluate himself in thc above way. Neither will a person who is a philosopher, and so on. Least of all one who is a painter! But the world evaluates all these matters today in this style in the social evaluation of human beings. And the end result is that a poet, let us say, has a net value of ten thousand francs for a publisher, if the publisher is generous from the time he begins to write his novel until it is finished. So, this is the value of a poet for a certain period of time, isn't that right? We have placed him also in the equalizing abstraction.

2. –	Fr. Butter
2 000 000. –	Fr. Madonna by Raffael
2.50	Fr. Toothbrush
–.70	Fr. Philosophical Work
10.–	Fr. Powder Box
10 000. –	Fr. Poet
3. –	Fr. Daily Capacity for Work

Well, I could cite all sorts of examples here; but I already said that the middle class didn't waste much time thinking about these matters. A poet in his attic room* – I am now referring to the "Oberstübchen" that is situated on a floor high above the others – naturally considers himself something quite special, but in social life he was worth ten thousand francs. But he paid no attention to that unless he happened to belong to the working class. He paid no heed to it. But the laborer did. From all this, he drew the conclusion: I don't have butter. I don't have powder. I don't have a philosophy book. But I do have my capacity for work. I offer it to the owner of the factory, and to him, it is worth, let's say, three francs for each day: the daily capacity for work.

You must forgive me for writing "poet" here for the reason that one could experience that a poet was treated a good deal worse in the course of the last few decades than the workman with his daily capacity for work. For the latter could defend himself still better than the poet, and as a rule, the ten thousand francs were not worth more than the wage of three francs for the proletarian working capacity, with the exception of a few. It goes without saying that poets such as, for example, the blessed E. Marlitt – I don't know if many of you remember her – earned splendid wages with her *The Secret of the Old Spinster*; a novel concerning which the best criticism would be the one expressed once by a certain person: Oh book, if only you had remained the secret of the old spinster!

Now the workman considered what he had become by having been placed into the abstraction of prices in regard to his capacity for work. For what does anything in the economic life represent by virtue of having a price tag? It is a commodity. Anything for which a price can be paid must be considered a commodity. I've said that the life of the middle class runs its course along with a certain indifference in regard to such matters. But these concepts arose from the working class and in this manner,

* Note by translator: Rudolf Steiner makes a pun with words here. The term "Oberstübchen" can refer in German to an attic room as well as one's head. Not to be quite right in the head can be expressed as not being quite right in the "Oberstübchen."

the idea emerged: We ourselves have become a commodity with our capacity for work.

This is something that now worked together with the other three concepts. A person who understands modern life correctly, knows that when he comprehends the four concepts, ideology, class consciousness, surplus value, capacity for work as a commodity in the right way so that he can place himself into life with these four concepts in regard to experiences, that he then encounters with these four concepts the reality of consciousness that exists in particular among the segment of the population that actively and consciously wants to bring about a transformation of social conditions. One therefore has the task of contemplating how to deal with these four concepts.

If a lecturer has a mixed audience of working-class people and those of the middle class, he will have to speak first of all in such a manner as to call attention to the fact that the working class could not help but arrive at these matters and how, due to modern life, a workman could not become acquainted with anything except the processes of the economic life. For this is how matters developed since approximately the middle of the fifteenth century. This was when it slowly began. For if we go back further than the middle of the fifteenth century, we find that man with his being was still connected with what he produced. One who makes a key pours his soul into his key. A shoemaker makes shoes with all his heart. And I am quite certain that among those, where these things continued on in a healthy way, no disdain existed in regard to any such labor. I am fully convinced – not only subjectively, for, if necessary, such matters could be proven – that Jakob Boehme* enjoyed producing his boots just as much as his philosophical works, his mystical texts that he wrote; likewise in the case of Hans Sachs,† for example. These matters – that something that is material is looked down upon, and that spiritual matters are overly valued – have only developed along with intellectualism and its abstractions in all

---

* *Jakob Boehme*, 1575-1624; mystic and shoemaker in Goerlitz.

† *Hans Sachs*, 1494-1576; *Meistersinger*, poet and shoemaker in Nuremberg.

areas. What happened is that through the modern economic life, which has been permeated by technology, the human being has been separated from his product so that no real love can any longer connect him with what he produces. Those people, who can still develop a sense of love for what they produce in certain professional fields, are becoming increasingly rare. Only in the so-called professions of the mind does this love still exist. This is what causes the unnatural element in social differences and even classifications in recent times. One has to go East – perhaps this is no longer possible now, but it was the case decades ago – in order to still find joy in one's profession. I must admit I was really delighted, actually moved, when, decades ago, I encountered a barber in Budapest to whom I had gone for a haircut, who danced around me all the time and each time when he had cut off something with his scissors, would say, taking his hand mirror: Oh what a wonderful cut I've just made! What a great cut this was! – Please go and try to find a barber capable of such enthusiasm today in our civilized country!

What has taken place is the separation of man from what he produces. It has become something of indifference to him. He is placed in front of a machine. What does he care about the machine! At most, it interests not even the one who built it, but only the one who invented it; and the interest that the inventor has in the machine is usually not a truly social interest. For social interest only begins when one can discover the possible value, the monetary yield, in other words, when the whole thing has been reduced to the level of its price.

It is, however, the economic life that the modern workman has become familiar with above all else. He has been placed into it. If he is to approach the spiritual life, the latter is nowhere connected with his immediate inner life. It does not move his soul. He accepts it as something alien, as ideology. It is part of the modern historical process that this ideology has developed.

If you are successful in calling forth a feeling in the workman that this is the case, however, then you have achieved the beginning of what has to be attained. For, a member of the working class listens to you today with the following attitude: It is an absolute necessity of nature that all art, all science, all religions are ideologies. He is very far from believing that with this view he has simply become the product of modern-day developments. It is very difficult to make that clear to him. If he does notice that everything is merely supposed to be ideology, he feels terrible about it and turns his whole way of thinking around; then he becomes aware of the completely illusory nature of this view. He of all people is, as it were, predisposed better than any other to feel disgust over the fact that everything has turned into ideology; but you must make him realize this in his feelings. The thoughts that you set forth or have developed in your own mind do not interest the listener. But in the way that I have described it, you lead him to the point of sensing the matter. For what is important is that you put the subject into the right light for workmen by giving your sentences this nuance.

For members of the middle class, the matter must be put in a different light again, for what is quite proper for people of the working class is detrimental for those of the middle class in this area. It is not only a matter of lecturing correctly, but due to the diversity of life today it is a matter of speaking well in the sense of what I said yesterday, and that as far as possible a lecturer addresses the members of the middle class as well. What has to be made clear to them is that, because they were indifferent to what was developing, they helped cause the problem. Because of what the middle class did, or rather didn't do, matters developed to the point where they have become ideology for the working class. Members of the middle class must be made to comprehend: Once upon a time, religion was something that filled the whole human being with an inner fire; it was something that gave rise to everything that a person carried out in the external world. Customs derived from what people considered holy in regard to social life. Art was something by means of which a human being rose above the hardships and difficulties of life on earth, and so on. But, oh, how the value of these spiritual properties has declined in the past few centuries! Because of the manner in which the middle class upholds them, the workman cannot experience them in any other way than as ideology.

Take the case where a workman comes into the office of the employer for whatever reason. He has his own views concerning the whole management of the business. Let's assume that the bookkeeper, to whom he was called, or the boss himself, has just left the office. The workman sees a large volume in which many entries are made. He has his own views concerning what the figures in it express. He has recently developed these views. Now, because the bookkeeper or the boss happens not to be there and he is half a minute early, he opens the cover and looks at the first page. There, it says on top of the page, "In God's name!" ("Mit Gott"). That catches his attention, for, indeed, this religious element appearing on the first page in the words, "In God's name," is really pure ideology, because the workman is convinced that there isn't much that is in "God's name" in the pages that follow. This is right in the style in which he pictures conditions in the world in general. There is as little truth in what people call religion, custom and so on as there is in this book, where it says "In God's name" on the first page. I don't know whether it says "In God's name" in ledgers in Switzerland; but it is quite common that people begin their account books with "In God's name."

Therefore, it is a matter of making clear to people of the middle class that they are the cause for the view concerning ideology among workmen.

Now, each party has its share. Then, the lecturer has reached the point where he can explain how the spiritual life must once again acquire reality, since it has in fact turned into ideology. If people have only ideas concerning the spirit and not the whole relationship with the actual spiritual life and substance, then this really is ideology. In this way one acquires a bridge to the sphere where a conception can be called forth concerning the reality of the spiritual life. Then it becomes possible to point out that the spiritual (cultural) life is a self-contained reality, not merely a product of the economic life, not just an ideology, but something real that is based on its own foundation. A feeling must be evoked for the fact that the spiritual life is a reality based on its own foundation. Such a self-evident reality is something other than an abstract fact, for something with an abstract basis must be based on a foundation elsewhere.

The workman claims that ideology is based on the economic life. But inasmuch as a person only abandons himself to abstract ideas in his spiritual life, this is indeed something ephemeral, something illusory. Only if people penetrate through this nebulous, illusory element, through the idea to the reality of the spiritual life – as happens by means of Anthroposophy – only then can the spiritual life be experienced as real once again. If the spiritual life is merely a sum of ideas, then these ideas do indeed stream up from the economic life. There, they have to be organized, there one has to provide them with an artificial effectiveness and order. And this is what the state has done. In the age when the spiritual life evaporated into ideology, the state took it in hand to bestow on it at least that reality, which people no longer experienced in the spiritual world itself.

This is how one must try to make it comprehensible in what way all this, which the state has given the spiritual life without being qualified to do so – since it has turned into ideology – does have a reality. It must have, after all, a reality. For if a person does not have legs of his own but wants to walk, he must have artificial ones made. In order to exist, any given thing must have reality. Therefore the spiritual life must have its own reality. This is what must be felt, namely, that the spiritual life must have its own reality.

To begin with, you will make a paradoxical impression among the people of the middle class as well as those of the working class. You must even call forth an awareness of the fact that you appear paradoxical. You can do this by giving rise to the conception among your listeners that you think in the same manner as the workman by making use of his language, and at the same time that you think like a member of the middle class by making use of his terminology. But then, after having developed these trains of thought that can be brought out with the help of what is recalled of experiences gained in life, after you have gone through something like this as a preparation, then you arrive at the point of speaking to people in such a way that gradually a comprehension can be brought about for the issues that must be met with understanding.

Speaking cannot be learned by means of external instructions. Speaking must be learned to a certain extent by means of understanding how to bring to the lecture the thinking that lies behind it, and the experience that lies before it, in a proper relationship.

Now, I have tried today to show you how the material first has to be dealt with. I have connected with what is known, in order to show you how the material should not be created out of some theory or other, how it must be drawn out of life, how it must be prepared so as to be dealt with in speaking. What I have said today everyone should now actually do in his own fashion as preparation for lecturing. Through such preparation the lecture gains forcefulness. Through thought preparation – preparing the organization of the lecture, as I have said at the beginning of today's remarks: from a thought that is then formed into a composition – the lecture becomes lucid, so that the listener can also receive it as a unity. What the lecturer brings along as thinking should not be woven into his own thoughts. Since, if he presents his own thoughts, they are, as I have already said, such as to interest no-one. Only through the use of one's own thinking in organizing the lecture does it become lucid, and through lucidity, comprehensible.

By means of the experiences that the lecturer should gather from everywhere (the worst experiences are still always better than none at all!) the lecture becomes forceful. If, for example, you tell some-one what happened to you, for all it matters, as you were going through a village where someone nearly gave you a box on the ear, then it is still always better if you judge life out of such an experience, than if you merely theorize. – Bring things out of experience, through which the lecture acquires blood, since through thinking it only has nerves. It acquires blood through experience, and through this blood, which comes out of experience, the lecture becomes forceful. Through the composition you speak to the under-standing of the listener; through your experience you speak to the heart of the listener. It is this which should be looked upon as a golden rule. Now, we can proceed step by step. Today I wanted more to show first of all in rough outline how the material can be transformed by degrees into what it afterwards has to be in the lecture. Tomorrow, then, we resume again at three o'clock.

Lecture 4

Yesterday I tried to describe how the first part of a lecture on the threefold social order could be dealt with in the case of a certain audience. I called attention to the fact that above all it is necessary to call forth a feeling for the special character of the spiritual life that stands independently on its own. In the second part it will be a matter of making it even comprehensible to present-day humanity that there can be something like a democratic-political connection that has to strive for equality. For it is actually a fact – and you must take this into consideration when preparing for such a lecture – that modern man has no feeling at all for a state structure that is built upon rights as upon its very foundation. This part, the political part referring to the state, is especially difficult to deal with within Swiss conditions. It will have to be specially emphasized that lecturers, who want to represent the threefold social order within Swiss conditions, proceed from the thus given Swiss conditions, and that in the middle part concerning the political, public life, they take into consideration how one must speak out of the Swiss context. After all, generally it is like this: Because of the conditions of the recent development of humanity, public life as such, which was to express itself in the life of rights, has in the main disappeared. What expresses and lives in the configuration of the state, is really a chaotic union of the spiritual elements of human existence and the economic elements. One could say that in the modern states the spiritual elements and the economic elements have gradually become mixed together; whereas the actual political life has fallen away in between, has in fact vanished.

This is particularly noticeable within the conditions of Switzerland. We are dealing there everywhere with a seeming democratization of the spiritual life, impossible in its actual formulations, and a democratization of economic life and the fact that the public believes that this apparent democratic mixture of the spiritual and the economic life is a democracy. Since people have formed their concepts of democracy out of this mixture, since they therefore have an absolute illusory concept of democracy, it is so difficult to speak of true democracy particularly to the Swiss. Actually, the Swiss know least of all about real democracy.

In Switzerland, one thinks about how to democratize the schools. This is about the same as if one were supposed to think about and gain an idea out of real, true concepts on how to turn a boot into a good head covering. The so-called democratic political concepts are treated in a similar manner. It serves no purpose to speak of these matters in a – let me say – pussy-footing manner in order to speak politely to a mainly Swiss audience; for then we could not understand each other. Politeness in such matters can never lead to an understanding. Well, just because of this it is so necessary to discuss the concept of rights and the equality of men in face of a people like the Swiss nation.

One has to accustom oneself to speak differently in each locality if one wants to be active as a lecturer. When, as was the case beginning in April 1919, one spoke about the threefold social order in Germany, one spoke under totally different conditions from those here in Switzerland, and also completely different conditions than those under which one can speak in England or in America about the threefold social order. Especially in that spring, in April 1919, directly after the German revolution, everybody in Germany, the proletarian as well as the middle class – the first naturally in a more revolutionary, the second in a more resigned manner – were convinced of the fact that something new would have to come. One actually spoke into this feeling, this mood, that something new had to come. One spoke at that time to relatively prepared, receptive people; naturally, one could speak in Germany quite differently from the way one could speak there today. A whole world lies between today and that spring of 1919 in Germany as well. Today, one can at most hope to call forth some sort of idea by means of something resembling the threefold social order of how the spiritual life as such can be structured independently – especially how it would have to be formulated under the conditions presently existing in Germany today, and how, under certain conditions, the inner-political life of rights within the state could be constituted. In Germany today, one naturally cannot speak of a formulation of the economic life completely in the sense of the threefold social order, for the economic life in Germany is in fact something that is under rules of duress, under pressure and such as that. It is something that cannot move freely, that cannot conceive ideas concerning its own free mobility. This is quite obvious in the completely different form of life of, for example, the Futurum and the Kommende Tag. The Kommende Tag exists as if in a straitjacket, and its task is to function under such conditions. The Futurum must work under Swiss conditions in the way it develops, conditions of which we shall speak further directly. Therefore, a speech must be formulated in different ways depending on whether it is delivered in Switzerland, Germany, or even at different times. Again, one would have to speak completely differently in England or in America. What can be accomplished from here, in Europe, in regard to these two countries, can only be a sort of substitute. It is alright, for example, if "The Threefold Social Order" is translated. It is fine if the book is widely distributed, but, as I have said from the beginning, in the final analysis the really effective way would be if the ideas of this book were set down in a totally different style for America and England. For both Switzerland and Central Europe, it can be taken literally word for word, the way it was written down. But for England and America the ideas would indeed have to be rendered in a completely different form because in those countries one addresses people who basically have the opposite attitude of what existed, for instance, among Germans in April of 1919. In Germany, the opinion prevailed that something new would have to come and to begin with, it would suffice, if one knew what this consisted of. One didn't have the mental strength to comprehend it but one had the feeling that one ought to know what this sensible innovation might be. Naturally, in all of England and America nothing like this feeling exists anywhere. The only concern there is how to hold on to and save the old traditions. The only worry is how to properly secure the past because the old values are good, so one thinks, and one must by no means shake the traditional foundations!

I am certainly aware that the above can be countered with the statement that there are so many progressive movements in the western hemisphere. Still, all these progressive movements, regardless of whether their inner content is new, are reactionary and conservative insofar as their management is concerned. The feeling that things cannot continue the way they have gone until now, has to be called into being over there in the West in the first place.

This can certainly be noticed by individual examples. Let us take a terrible, horrible, I could say the worst problem that could have arisen from a purely human standpoint, the question of starvation in Russia. Although the views are ever so chaotic within Germany, even though for reasons of agitation one acts contrary to what would be sensible, and although, out of humane reasons, homage is paid to pity in a matter-of-fact manner – and naturally, we are not saying anything against pity holding sway – within Germany, at least in some circles, one is finally more or less reaching the conclusion that it is nonsense for the whole course of humanity's evolution to do something for the starvation of Russia in the form of subsidies, by gifts, as it were, from the West. People are getting the idea that this is quite certainly demanded even from a humane standpoint, but that what is done in this direction is so self-evident that nobody should say that it has anything to do with the tasks posed today by the starvation conditions in Russia. In the West, only a few theorists – but then only on the basis of something theoretical – might arrive at such views. It is therefore natural that one must first call forth a feeling in the West for the fact that the world needs a new form, a reformation.

Switzerland's position during the dreadful catastrophe of recent times (the First World War) was such that it only participated in a theoretical way, namely by means of journalistic theory in the events, also by means of what influenced the cultural and economic conditions from outside. The Swiss population therefore has no actual feeling at all, neither of the fact that something new should come into being, nor that the old ought to remain. If today, depending on one or the other party consideration, a Swiss person speaks about something new having to come into being, or something old having to remain, one has the feeling that he only tells one what he has heard, heard on the one hand from Central Europe, on the other from England and the West. He only speaks of what has reached his ears, not of what he has actually experienced. This is why it appears so like the Swiss, when those individuals who don't like to engage themselves to the right or to the left – and leading Swiss are very often like this today – that such people say: Well, when this happens, it happens in this way, and when the other takes place, it occurs that way! If something new comes into being, matters take their course thusly, if the old remains, matters run that way! One figures out, as it were, what one must put on one or the other side of the scale.

It is like this: When one tries to make somebody in Switzerland take an interest in something that is bitterly needed for the world today, one can become quite desperate, for it doesn't really move him at all, for it bounces right back because in reality his heart is not in it. It is too distasteful to him for him to become interested, and he has too little experience concerning these matters for them to be-come in some way appealing to his sympathy. He wants to have his peace. On the other hand, he wants to be a Swiss. This signifies: If all sorts of progressive reports that include "freedom" and "democracy" resound across the border, and since one has through many centuries called oneself democratic, one cannot turn around and say that one doesn't want democracy! In short, one really has the feeling that people in Switzerland have an exceedingly well-built canal between the right and the left ear, so that everything that goes in one side goes out on the other without having reached common sense and the heart.

One will have to at least take hold at those points where it can be shown that a political system like that of Switzerland is really something quite special. It is indeed something quite special. For, first of all, Switzerland is something like a center of gravity of the world – which was already noticeable during the war, if one wanted to take notice of it. Particularly its non-alliance in regard to the various world conditions could be utilized by Switzerland to achieve free, independent judgment and actions in regard to its surroundings. The world is literally waiting for the Swiss to note in their heads what they note in their pockets. In their pockets they notice that the franc has not been affected by the rise and fall and corruption of currency. The Swiss realize that the whole world revolves around the Swiss franc. That this is also the case in a spiritual regard is something the Swiss don't notice at all. Just as they know how to value the unchanging franc, which, as it were, has become the regulator of currency the world over, the Swiss should learn to understand their independent position, brought about by world conditions, whereby Switzerland could indeed be a kind of lever for world conditions. It is therefore necessary that one makes this comprehensible to them.

It is almost similar to the way one had to speak at one time about Austria. People who knew something about such matters in Austria have often pondered the question why this Austria, which only had centrifugal tendencies, remained in existence, why it didn't split apart. In the 1880's and in the '90's, I never said anything else but: What occurs in Austria itself has to begin with no significance for the cohesiveness or the splitting apart (of the state structure), what happens around it, does. Because the others – Germany, Russia, Italy, Turkey, and those interested in Turkey, France and Switzerland itself – because these political systems that surround Austria on all sides do not let Austria split apart, and instead hold it centrally together for the reason that each (country) begrudged the other a part of it! Each took pains that the other would not acquire anything. By these means Austria held together. It was held together from outside. One could clearly see this if one had an eye for such things. Only when this mutual watch of the surrounding powers was obscured in the World War by the smoke of the cannons, only then did Austria naturally split apart. Basically, this picture says it all.

Well, it is similar in the case of Switzerland, yet it is different. All around, there are all sorts of diverse interests, but these interests left out one small spot where they do not confront each other. And today, where there is the life of the world economy, of the cultural life, matters are such that this small spot is maintained by virtue of being something quite special. What does it represent? It is something that is held together within its borders by purely political conditions. You can see this from the history of Switzerland. Swiss history is seemingly completely political, just as Swiss thinking is seemingly completely democratic. It is the same, however, in politics in Switzerland as I explained it earlier concerning democracy. It is a form of politics that is no politics; on a small spot of the world it governs the cultural and the economic life, but in reality is not politically active. Compare what is politics in Switzerland and what it is elsewhere! Occasionally, one or the other matter must be done in a political sense, because one must enter into correspondence with other countries. But genuine Swiss politics – you would have to turn things upside-down, if you wanted to discover real Swiss politics. That doesn't really exist. But this makes it evident that here a national configuration was created in which the cultural and the economic life are governed in a political sense, but in which there actually does not exist a true feeling, a true experience of the existence of rights.

Therefore, it is a matter of especially emphasizing here that rights are something that cannot be defined, as red or blue cannot be defined, and that rights need to be experienced in their self-evident quality, something that must be experienced when a person, who has become of age, becomes conscious of himself as a human being. Therefore, it would be a matter of trying to work out this human relationship of feelings and sensations in the life of rights, in the political life for Swiss conditions, to show that equality must dwell in the individual person if there is to be a life of rights. For it is Switzerland that is actually called upon – and I would like to say that the angels of the whole world look upon Switzerland to watch whether the right things take place here, – to create a system of rights by letting go, freeing the cultural and the economic life. For, Switzerland is, if I may put it this way, quite virginal in regard to the political life.

Roman jurisprudence, which moved in a quite different way into France and Germany and the other European countries, was really stopped by the Swiss mountains from entering people's hearts. It only moved into external elements, not into people's feelings. Therefore, this is virginal soil for rights, soil on which everything can be created. If only people will come to the realization what infinite good luck it signifies to be able to live here between the mountains, to be able to have a will of their own, independent of the whole world that revolves around this tiny country! Just because of world conditions, the elements of rights can be brought out here, worked purely out of the human being.

Now I have indicated to you how one must take into consideration the particular locality, the specific area for the preparations of such a lecture, how one must be completely sure within oneself about what the essence of the Swiss character is. Naturally, I can only outline it now; but anybody who wants to lecture in Switzerland should really try hard to fully understand what specific form the Swiss character consists of.

Now it is true, you might say: We are, after all, Swiss – just as the English could say we are English – and you want to tell us how a Swiss is to become acquainted with the Swiss character, and what all an Englishman might not have of such feelings, and so on. Certainly, one can say that. But those who belong today to the educated class have no truly experienced education, no education that has emerged out of direct experience. This is the reason why, especially in reference to rights, this direct experience must be specifically pointed out.

With this we arrive at a consideration of how human beings have gradually come into social relationships in modern civilization in the area where rights should really develop. Rights should develop from person to person. Anything else, all parliamentary debates, are basically only a surrogate for what should take its course from one person to the next in a truly correct realm of rights.

If one now ponders the area of rights, one has the opportunity – but now in a more realistic manner – to go into what the concepts of the proletariat consist of and the feelings of the bourgeois. But now, one can lead what the proletariat has developed in its concepts in a more realistic way into the feelings of the bourgeois. I say: concepts of the proletariat, feelings of the bourgeois. You can find the explanation for it in my *Towards Social Renewal*.

Out of the four concepts that I developed here yesterday, the proletariat has certainly evolved the feeling of class consciousness; it must appropriate what is in the possession of the bourgeois, namely the state. To what extent the state is a true state of rights or not is something that did not become clear naturally to the proletariat either. But what has developed as a state of rights is something that Switzerland has least of all been touched by; therefore it could comprehend a true state of rights most readily without any prejudices. What has developed as a real state of rights actually lives only between the expressions of the main soul life of people almost the world over today, but not in Switzerland! Everywhere else in the world, the element that is the political state of rights lives an underground existence, so to speak, whereas the element that is really experienced between person and person is based on some-thing quite different, namely on something that is through and through a middle-class element. What man actually seeks in public life, what he carries into the whole of public life, whereby an obscuring of the actual life of rights takes place for him – that is something that one can only grasp if one focuses a bit on the concrete relationships.

You see, the cultural, the spiritual, life has gradually been absorbed by the life of the state (the government). The cultural life, however, when one confronts it as an element standing on its own ground, is a very stern element, an element in regard to which one must constantly preserve one's freedom, which therefore cannot be organized in any other way except in freedom. Just let one generation unfold its spiritual life more freely and then organize it any way it wants to: it will be purest slavery for the following generation. Not only according to theory, but according to life, the spiritual, cultural life must really be free. The human beings who stand within it must experience this freedom. The cultural life turns into a great tyranny if it spreads out anywhere on earth, for without being organized it cannot spread, and when organization occurs, the organization itself becomes a tyrant. Therefore, there must be a constant battle in freedom, in living freedom, against the tyranny to which the cultural life is inclined.

Now, in the course of the nineteenth century, the cultural life has been absorbed by the life of the state. This means: If one divests the life of the state of the toga in which it is still very much clothed in memory of the ancient Roman age – although judges are even beginning to discard the robe, but all in all one can still say that the life of the state still wears the toga – if one disregards this toga, looks instead at what is real, one sees everywhere the constrained spiritual life that is present in the state and the social life of the state. It is the restrained spiritual life! It is constrained but ignorant of the fact that it is constrained; therefore it does not strive for freedom, although it does constantly fight against its constraint. Much has emerged in recent times out of this fighting against the constraint of spiritual life. Our whole public cultural life really stands under the influence of this constraint of cultural life, and we cannot attain to healthy social conditions if we do not acquire a feeling for awareness of this constraint. One must have a feeling for how this constraint of the spiritual life meets one in everyday life.

One day, I was invited by a number of ladies in Berlin, who had heard lectures of mine in an institute, to give a lecture in the private apartment of one of these ladies. The whole arrangement was really for the purpose of the ladies' working against a certain relatively harmless attitude of their husbands. You see, the ladies arrived around twelve o'clock noon in the institute where I gave my lectures. When such a day recurred – I think it was once a week – the husbands said, "There you go again into your crazy institute today; then the soup will be bad again, or something else won't be in its usual order!" So the ladies wanted me to give a lecture on Goethe's *Faust* – this was selected as the subject – the husbands were also invited. Now I gave the lecture on Goethe's *Faust* before the ladies and gentlemen. The men were a bit perplexed afterwards and said, "Why yes, but Goethe's *Faust* is a science; Goethe's *Faust* is not art. Art, well that's Blumenthal* " – I am quoting word for word – "and there one doesn't have to make such an effort. After working so hard in our professional life, who wants to exert an effort in our leisure time!" You see, what has become a substitute for enthusiasm for freedom in cultural life confronts us in the social life as a mere desire to be lightly entertained.

In the countryside, where one could still observe this well, I once saw how these old traveling actors, who always had a clown among them, sometimes presented really fine acts. I watched how the clown, who had been doing his clownish acts for some time and had entertained the people with them, threw off the clown's costume, because he now wanted to act out something that was serious to him. And there he stood in black trousers and black tails. This image always turns itself around in my mind: First I see the man in his formal black attire. Afterwards I see the man in his clown's costume. To me it's like black trousers and tails when, somewhere in a window display, I see a book by Einstein about the theory of relativity; and I see a clown, when, next to it, I have before me a book by Moszkowski on the theory of relativity. For, indeed, there is much that's maya in outer life. But one couldn't imagine that the whole pedantry of thinkers could inwardly appear other than in black trousers and well-cut tails, I mean in the theory of relativity. And again: It is bothersome to adjust to such stern processes of thinking, such consistent sequences of thoughts, which are really cut like a well-fitting formal suit; that must confront people in a different manner as well. So, Alexander Moszkowski, especially gifted feuilletonistically as a philosopher-clown, gets busy and writes a voluminous book. From it, all the people learn in the form of light literature in the clown's costume, what was born in coat and tails! You see, one cannot do other than translate things into

---

* *Oskar Blumenthal*, 1852-1917; author of light comedy.

something that requires no effort and where no great enthusiasm need be engendered.

It is namely this overall mood that must be opposed in people's feelings, if one wants to speak about concepts of rights, for there, the human being with all his inner worth confronts the other person as an equal. What does not allow the concepts of rights to arise, is – to put it this way – the Alexander-Moszkowski element. One must seek for the concrete facts in any given situation.

Naturally, I am not saying that if one needs to speak of concepts of human rights, one has to talk about tails and clowns' costumes. But I would like to show how one has to possess an elasticity of concepts in all matters, how one has to point out both sides of a question, and how one's own mind needs to be disposed in order to gain the necessary fluency to lecture to people.

There is another reason why a modern lecturer must be aware of such things as these. Most of the time, he is compelled to speak in the evening, when he wants to present something important concerning the future, for example. This means that he has to make use of the time when people prefer to attend either the theater or a concert. Therefore, the lecturer must realize that he is speaking to an audience that, according to the mood of the hour, would be better off in the concert hall, the theater, or another place of entertainment. So the audience is really in the wrong place if it finds itself in a lecture hall listening to a speaker who discourses from the platform on some important topic. As a speaker, one must be aware of what one is doing, down to the last detail.

What does one in fact accomplish when forced to address such an audience? Quite literally, one ruins the listener's digestion! A serious speech has the peculiar effect of negatively reacting on the stomach juices, on pepsin. A serious lecturer causes stomach acidity. And only if the speaker is in the proper frame of mind to permeate his address at least inwardly with the necessary humor, can the digestive juices function harmoniously after all. One has to present a speech with a certain inner lightness, modulation, and with an amount of enthusiasm, then one aids the processes of digestion. This way, the adverse effects on people's stomachs, caused by the time of day when one is normally forced to lecture, are neutralized. One is not promoting social ideas but instead medical specialists if one speaks pedantically, with heavy, expressive emphasis. The style must be light and matter-of-fact, or else one does not further the ideas of the threefold social order but the medical specialist's practice! There are no statistics available about the number of people who end up at the doctor's office after they have listened to pedantic speeches, but if there were, one would be astonished at the percentage of people among patients of gastro-intestinal specialists who are eager listeners of lectures nowadays.

I must draw attention to these facts because the time is near when one must be familiar with the actual constitution of the human being. We must know how seriousness or humor affects the stomach and the digestive juices; how, for example, wine acts like a cynic who does not take the human organism seriously but plays with it, as it were. If the human organization were to be viewed with human concepts rather than with the confused, indecisive concepts of today's science, one would certainly realize how every word and word relationship causes an organic, almost chemical, reaction in the human being.

Knowing such things makes lecturing easier too. The barrier that otherwise stands between speaker and audience ceases to exists if one becomes aware of the damage that a pedantic speech causes the stomach. One frequently has occasion to observe that; though that is less the case in a lecture class at a university, there, the students protect themselves by not paying attention!

From all this, one can readily understand how much depends on the mood in lecturing. It is much more important to prepare the whole mood-atmosphere and have it in hand than to get the speech ready word for word. A person who has prepared himself for the correct mood need not concern himself with the verbal details to a point where, at a given moment, the latter would cause the listeners discomforts.

Several different aspects go into the makeup of a correctly trained speaker. I want to mention this at this particular point because a discussion of justice, of rights, demands much that has to be characterized in this direction. I want to bring this out now before I shall talk tomorrow about the relationship of speaking and the economic elements.

An anthroposophist once brought the well-known philosopher, Max Dessoir (1867-1947), along to an evening lecture I was giving at the Architektenhaus in Berlin. This one-time friend of Max Dessoir's said afterwards, "Oh, that Dessoir didn't go along with the lecture after all! I asked him how he had liked it and he replied that he was a public speaker himself; therefore, being one himself, he could not listen properly and form a judgment about what another lecturer was saying." Well, I did not have to form a judgment about Dessoir following this statement. I had other opportunities for that. Indeed, I wouldn't have done so based on this utterance because I couldn't be sure whether it was really the truth or whether Dessoir, as usual, had lied here too. But assuming it was the truth, what would it have proven? It would have been proof that a person holding such an opinion could never be a proper speaker. A person can never become a good speaker if he enjoys speaking, likes to hear himself talk, and attaches special importance to his own talks. A good speaker always has to experience a certain reluctance when he has to speak. He must clearly feel this reluctance. Above all, he should much prefer listening to another speaker, even the worst one, to speaking himself.

I know very well what I imply with this statement and I realize how difficult it is for some of you to believe me in this, but it is so. Of course, I concede that there are better things to do in life than to listen to poor speakers.

But one's own speaking must by no means be included among the better things! Instead, one has to feel a certain urge to hear others, even enjoy listening to others. It is not love for his own speeches but listening to others that makes a person into a good speaker. A certain fluency is acquired by speaking but this has to happen instinctively. What makes one a speaker is basically listening, the development of an ear for the specific peculiarities of the other orators, even if they are poor ones. Therefore, I tell anybody who asks me how to best prepare to become a good speaker, to listen to and to read the speeches of others! Only by doing this does one acquire a strong feeling of distaste for one's own speaking. And this distaste is the very thing that enables one to speak realistically. This is extremely important. And if people are as yet unsuccessful in viewing their own speeches with antipathy, it is good if they at least retain their stage fright. To stand up and lecture without stage fright and with sympathy for one's own speech is something that ought not to be done because, under any circumstances, the results thus achieved would be negative. It contributes to rigidity, petrification and lack of communication in speech and belongs to the elements that ruin the sermon!

I would indeed not be speaking in the spirit of the aims of this speech course if I would enumerate on rules of speech to you taken from some old book on rhetoric or copied from dusty rhetorical speeches. Instead, from my own living experience I want you to take to heart what one should always have in mind when one wants to influence one's fellowmen by lecturing.

Things change quite a bit if one is forced into a debate. In a sense, a certain rights-relationship between person and person comes up in a discussion. But in the debate through which one can learn most beautifully about human rights, the projection of general concepts of rights into the relationship existing between two people in a discussion hardly plays a role today. Yet here it is indeed important not to be in love with one's own way of thinking and feeling.

Instead, in a debate one should feel antipathy for one's own reaction and replies. Because then, by suppressing one's own opinion, annoyance or excitement, one can instead project oneself into the other person's mind. Thus, even if one has to take exception to something in a debate, this attitude has positive results. Of course one cannot simply reiterate what the partner has stated but one can take the substance of an effective rebuttal from understanding him in the first place.

An example that best illustrates this point is the following exchange that took place in the German Parliament between the delegate Rickert and Chancellor Bismarck. Rickert gave a speech in which he accused Bismarck of changing the direction of his political leanings. He pointed out that Bismarck had gone along with the Liberals for a time and then had changed to the Conservatists. He summed it all up with the metaphor that Bismarck's politics amounted to trimming his sails to the wind. One can imagine what an effect such a statement had in a place where everybody is ready to talk! Bismarck, however, rose and with a certain air of superiority, to begin with, presented what he had to say in reply to Rickert's remarks. And then, projecting himself into the other like he always did in similar cases, he said, "Rickert has accused me of trimming my sails to the wind. But politics is somewhat like navigating a ship on sea. I would like to know how one can hold a steady course if one does not adjust to the wind. A real pilot, like a successful politician, must certainly adjust to the wind in steering his course – unless, possibly, he wants to make wind himself!"

One sees that this metaphor is put to use, turned in such a direction that the verbal arrow hits back at the archer. In a debate it is a matter of picking up the points made by the opponent and quite seriously using them to counter him. Thus, one undoes him with his own arguments. As a rule it doesn't help much if one simply sets one's own reasons against those of the opponent.

In a debate one should he able to evoke the following mood: The moment the debate begins one should he in a position to turn off everything one knew up to now, push it down into one's subconscious mind, and retain only what the speaker, whom one has to reply to, has said. Then one can properly exercise one's talent of setting straight what the other speaker said. Setting matters straight is what's important! In a discussion it is important to take up directly what the other has said, not to oppose him with something one knew some time ago. If one does that, as happens in most debates, the end result will indeed be inconclusive and fruitless. One has to realize that in a discussion one can never successfully argue the opponent down. One can only demonstrate that he either contradicts himself or reality. One can only go into what he has set forth. If this attitude is developed as the basic rule for debates it will be of great significance for them. If a person only wants to bring out in a debate what he has known previously, then it will certainly be of no significance that he does so after the opponent has stated his case.

I once experienced a most instructive illustration of the above. During my last trip to Holland, I was invited to give a lecture before the Philosophical Society of the University of Amsterdam. Of course, the chairman there had a different opinion from mine already, no doubt about that! And if he participated in the debate he would differ from my viewpoints greatly. But it was equally clear that whatever he would have to say would have no effect on my lecture, and that my views would have no special influence on what he would say based on what he had known beforehand. Therefore, I thought that he was quite clever. He brought out what he had to say not afterwards, during the debate, but before my lecture. What he did add later to what he had said at the start might just as well have been said at the beginning too. It wouldn't have changed matters one bit.

One shouldn't have any illusions concerning such things. It is most important that an orator be very, very strongly attuned to human relationships. But, if matters are to have results, one cannot afford having illusions about human relations. And as a foundation for the following lectures, let me say that, above all, one should have no illusions about the effectiveness of speeches.

I always find it extremely humorous when well-meaning people say all the time that words don't matter, deeds do! I've heard it proclaimed at the most unsuitable times, during discussions and from the rostrums, that it isn't words but actions that count!

Everything that happens in the world in regard to actions depends on words! One who can see through things knows that nothing takes place that hasn't been prepared in advance by somebody through words.

But one will understand that this preparation is a subtle, delicate process. If it is true that theoretical, pedantic speaking affects the digestion, one can imagine how indigestion in turn affects actions, and how public actions are the results of such poor speeches. And if, on the other hand, speakers try to be humorists and only act funny, this results in an overproduction of digestive juices that act like vinegar. And vinegar is a terrible hypochondriac. But the general public is constantly entertained by what flows through public life as continuous fun-making. The jokes of yesterday are not yet digested when the fun of today makes its appearance. And so, the digestive juices turn into something like vinegar. Oh, man is already being entertained again today and maybe he is quite cheerful about it. But the way he places himself into public life is influenced by the hypochondria of this vinegar-like substance at work in him.

One must know how the dimension of speaking fits into the world of actions. The most untrue expression concerning speaking, born of a false sentimentality that is in itself wrong, is,

> The words you've bandied are sufficient;
> 'Tis deeds that I prefer to see ...
>
> (From *Faust*, Prelude on Stage)

Certainly, this can be said in a dramatic play, and rightly so in its place. But when it is taken out of context and made into a general dictum, it might be true but it certainly will not be good. And we should learn to speak not only beautifully or correctly but effectively as well, so that good will come of it. Otherwise, we lead people into the abyss and can certainly never speak to them about anything that has lasting value for the future.

Lecture 5

I have tried to characterize how one can formulate a lecture on the threefold social order from out of *one* thought, and then arrange it in sections. What one can generally say concerning the whole social organism, as well as references to what can occur in the first two realms – namely that of the spiritual life and that of the judicial, the body politic – was contained in what I said. You will have understood from that, how, preparing oneself for the content of such a lecture, one can proceed.

Now, one can also prepare oneself for the form of delivery by immersing oneself into the thoughts and feelings. We shall perhaps understand each other best if I say that the preparation should be such that we try hard first to sense and then to utter what is related to the spiritual life in a more lyrical language (without, of course, resorting to singing, recitation, or some such thing), in a lyrical manner of speech, with quiet enthusiasm, so that one demonstrates through the way of delivering the matters that everything one has to say concerning the spiritual life comes from out of oneself. One should by all means call forth the impression that one is enthusiastic about what one envisions for the spiritual part of the social organism. Naturally, it must not be false, mystical, sentimental enthusiasm, a made-up enthusiasm. We achieve the right impression if we prepare ourselves first in imagination, in inner experience – even so far as to modulation – how, approximately, something like that could be said. I say specifically how, approximately, something like that could be said, because we should never commit ourselves word for word; rather what we prepare is, in a sense, a speech taking its course only in inward thoughts; and we are certainly ready to reformulate what we finally come out and say.

But when we speak about rights-relationships, we should make the attempt to speak dramatically. That implies: when we lecture about the equality of men, discussing it by means of examples, we should try as much as possible to put ourselves into the other person's position with our thinking. For instance, we should call to mind the image of how a person who seeks work, asserts his right to work in the sense of *Kernpunkte der sozialen Frage* (*The Threefold Social Order*). By making it evident that on one hand we are speaking from the other person's position, from out of his assertion of rights, we should then make it evident how through a slight change in the tone of voice we pass on to the topic of how one ought to meet such an assertion out of general humanitarian reasons. So it is dramatic speaking, very strongly modulated, dramatic lecturing, that calls forth the impression in listeners that one could think one's way into the souls of other persons; that is the manner we should employ in speaking about the rights- relationships.

When lecturing on economic conditions, the main point is that we speak directly from experience. If, in the spirit of the threefold social organism, one speaks about economic relationships, one should not permit the belief to arise that there even could be such a thing as a theoretical political economy. Instead, one should limit the main discussion to describing cases taken from the economic life itself; either cases that one repeats, or cases that one construes as to how they should be or could be. But with the latter cases – saying how they should or could be – one must never neglect to speak out of economic experience. Actually, when lecturing on the economic life, one should speak in an epic style. Particularly, when presenting what is written in the *Kernpunkte*, one should speak as if one had no preconceived ideas at all concerning the economic life, and had no notions that this should be thus and so; instead, one should speak as if one were informed on all and everything by the facts themselves.

One can evoke a certain feeling, for example, that it is correct to permit the transfer of the administration of monetary funds from one who is not involved in it himself anymore, to somebody who once again can participate in it. But one can only speak about something like that if one presents it to people by means of descriptions of what takes place if there are legacies merely due to blood relationships, or what can take place when such a transfer is occasioned in the way it is described in the *Kernpunkte*. Only by placing such a matter before people in a living way, as if one were copying reality, can one speak in such a way that the speech truly stands within the economic life. And just in this way, one can make the idea of "associations"* comprehensible and plausible. One will make it plausible that an individual person really knows nothing about the economic life; that if he wants to arrive at a judgment as to what must be done in the life of the economy, he is basically completely dependent on communicating with others. A sound economic view can only emerge from groups of people and one is therefore dependent on associations.

Then, one will perhaps meet with comprehension if one calls attention to the fact that much of what exists today actually came out of ancient, instinctive associations. Just consider for a moment how today's abstract market brings things together, whose combination and redistribution to the consumer cannot be surveyed at all. But how has one arrived at this market relationship in the first place? Basically, from the instinctive association of a number of villages located around a larger township, at a distance that one could travel back and forth on foot in one day, where people exchanged their products. One did not call that an association. One did not coin any word for it, but in reality it was an instinctive association. Those people who here came together for the market were associated with all of those who lived in the surrounding villages. They could count on a set circulation of goods that resulted from experience. Therefore they could regulate production according to consumption in truly living relationships. There certainly existed such associative conditions in such primitive economies; they just didn't call themselves that.

All this has become impossible to oversee, with the enlargement of the economic territories. In particular, it has become senseless in regard to the world economy. The world economy that has come into being only in the last third of the 19th Century, has reduced everything into an abstract realm; that is, it has reduced everything in the economic life to the

---

* See *The Threefold Social Order* for details on "Associations."

turnover of money or its monetary value, until this reduction has proven its own absurdity.

Indeed, when Japan fought a war with China and Japan won the war, one could very simply pay the war reparations by way of the Chinese Minister's handing a check to the Japanese Delegate, which the latter then deposited in a bank in Japan. This is an actual course of events. There were values contained in this check, which is money and has monetary value. It represented values. If you imagine how at that time everything should have been transported from one territory into the other this would have been a difficult process under modern-day conditions. But owing to the manner in which Japan and China were placed within the whole world economy, it could be done this way. However, all this has led itself to a point of absurdity. In the dealings between Germany and France, it has proven itself to be impossible.* I am therefore of the opinion that the state of affairs can best be explained out of the economic relationships themselves, and then one can explain the necessity for the associative principle.

Once again, one should have to divide this subject matter regarding the economic life in a certain way, and one would have to pass on to several concluding sentences of which I have already said that they again should be conceived verbatim or at least almost word for word.

So, how will the preparation for a speech appear, in fact? Well, one should try one's best to get into the situation or the subject that the audience is prepared for, by formulating the opening sentences in a way one considers necessary. One will have greater difficulty in the case of completely unprepared listeners; less difficulty, if one addresses a group that one finds already involved in the matter, at least possessing the corresponding feelings concerning the assertions one makes. Then, one will neither write down the rest of the speech nor jot down mere catch words. Experience shows that neither the verbatim

---

* Rudolf Steiner refers here to the war-reparations demanded of Germany by France.

composition nor the mere noting down of catch words leads to a good speech. The reason for not writing down the speech is because it ties one down and easily causes embarrassment when the memory falters; this is most frequently the case when the speech is written down word for word. Catch words easily mislead one to formulate the whole preparation too abstractly. On the other hand, if one needs to have such a support, what one should best write down and bring along as notes are a number of correctly formulated sentences that serve as catch phrases. They do not make the claim that one delivers them in the same way as a part of the speech; instead, they indicate: first, second, third, fourth, and so on; they are extracts, so to speak, so that from one sentence perhaps ten or eight or twelve will result. But one should write such sentences down. One should therefore not write down, "spiritual life conceived as independent"; instead, "The spiritual life can only thrive if it freely works independently out of itself." (Catch phrases, in other words.) If you do something like this, you will then have the experience yourself that owing to such catch phrases, you can in a relatively short time most readily attain to a certain facility of speaking freely, a speaking that only contains the ladder of catch phrases.

Concerning the conclusion, it is often very good if, in a certain sense, at least gently, one leads back to the beginning; if therefore the end, in a sense, contains something that, as a theme, was also contained in the beginning.

And then, such catch phrases readily give one the opportunity to really prepare oneself in the way indicated above by having noted these sentences down on a piece of paper. So, let us say, one ponders the following: what you have to say for the spiritual life must have a sort of lyrical nature within you; what you have to say concerning the rights relationships must have a kind of dramatic character in your mind; and what concerns the economic life must live in your mind in a narrative, epic form; a quiet, narrative, epic character. Then, the desire, as well as the skill, to word the catch phrases in the formulation that I have indicated, will indeed begin to arise instinctively. The preparation will result quite instinctively in such a way that the manner in which one speaks merges indeed into what one has to say concerning the subject. For this it is necessary, however, to have brought one's command of language to the level of instinct, so that one indeed experiences the speech organs the way one would, for instance, feel the hammer, if one wanted to use the hammer for something. That can be achieved, if one practices a little speech-gymnastics.

It's true, isn't it, that when one practices gymnastics, those are not movements that are later executed in real life; they are movements that make one flexible and dexterous. Similarly, one should make the speech organs pliable and adroit; but making the latter pliable and dexterous is something that must be accomplished so that it goes together with the inner soul life, and so that one learns to be aware of the sound in speaking. In the seminar courses that I held over two years ago in Stuttgart for the Waldorf School teachers, I put together a number of such speech exercises that I now want to pass on to you. They are mostly of a kind that, by their content, does not prevent one from learning to merge oneself purely into the element of speech; they are only designed for practicing speech-gymnastics. If one tries again and again to say these sentences aloud, but in such a way that one always probes: how does one best use his tongue, how does one best use his lips so as to produce this particular sequence of sounds? – then one makes oneself independent of speaking and, instead, places that much more value on mental preparation for lecturing.

I shall now read you a number of such sentences whose content is often senseless, but whose purpose is to make the speech organs pliable and fit for public speaking.*

Dass er dir log, uns darf es nicht loben.
(That he told lies, 'it' is not to be lauded.)

This is the easiest one. Something a bit more complicated:

---

* The speech-exercises are rendered in the original German, since the emphasis is primarily on their sound, a translation is often useless as well as extremely difficult.

Nimm nicht Nonnen in nimmermüde Mühlen.
(Take not nuns in never-tired mills.)

One should try increasingly, along with the sequence of sounds, to make the organs of speech pliable; to bend, to hollow, to take possession of them.†

Another example:

Rate mir mehrere Rätsel nur richtig.

It is naturally not enough to say something like this once, or ten times; but again and again and again, because even if the speech organs are already pliable, they can become still more so.

An example that I consider to be particularly useful is the following:

Redlich ratsam
Rüstet rühmlich
Riesig rächend
Ruhig rollend
Reuige Rosse

With this, one has the opportunity to regulate the breath in the pauses, something one has to pay attention to and that can be particularly well done through such an exercise. In a similar way, not all the letters, nor all the sounds, have the same value for this practice. You make progress if you take the following, for example:

Protzig preist
Bäder brünstig
Poltend putzig
Bieder bastelnd
Puder patzend
Bergig brüstend

---

† In trying to illustrate how one must take hold of one's speech-organs via the exercises, Rudolf Steiner modifies the four words in a manner that is highly original and unusual, and untranslatable as well. But they thus indicate a living working, an active doing. *Geschmeidigen*, to make pliable; *zu biegen*, to bend; *zu hohlen*, to make hollow; *zu erhabenen*, to have or possess by effort.

If you succeed in finding your way into this sequence of sounds, you gain much from it.

When one has done such exercises, then one can also try to do those exercises that cannot but result in bringing a mood into the speaking of the sounds. I have tried to give an example of how the sounds can pour into the mood in the following:

Erfüllung geht (Fulfillment goes)
Durch Hoffnung (Through hope)
Geht durch Sehnen (Goes through longing)
Durch Wollen (Through will)

and now it passes more into the sounds, through which, here in particular, the mood in the sound itself is held fast:

Wollen weht (Willing wafts)
Im Webenden (In weaving)
Weht im Bebenden (Wafts in billowing)
Webt bebend (Weaves billowing)
Webend bindend (Weaves binding)
Im Finden (In finding)
Findend windend (Finding winding)
Kündend (Calling)

You will always discover, when you do these exercises in particular, how you are able, without letting the breath disturb you, to regulate the breathing by simply holding yourself onto the sounds. In recent times, one has thought up all kinds of more or less clever methods for breathing and for all kinds of accompanying aspects of speaking and singing, but actually, all of those are no good, because speech with everything that belongs with it, with the breath, too, should by all means be learned through actual speaking. This implies that one should learn to speak in such a way that, within the boundaries that result from the sound sequence and the word relationships, the breath also regulates itself as a matter of course. In other words, one should only learn breathing during speech – in speaking itself. Therefore, the exercises of speech should be so designed that, in correctly feeling them regarding their sounds, one is obliged – not by the content but by the sounds – to formulate the breath correctly because one experiences the sound correctly.

What the verse below represents, points once again to the content of the mood. It has four lines; these four lines are arranged so that they are an ascent, as it were. Each line causes an expectation, and the fifth line is the conclusion and brings fulfillment. Now one should really make an effort to execute this speech movement that I have just characterized. The verse goes like this:

In den unermesslich weiten Räumen,
In den endenlosen Zeiten,
In der Menschenseele Tiefen,
In der Weltenoffenbarung:
Suche des grossen Rätsels Lösung.

(In the unmeasurably wide realms,
in the never-ending ages,
in the human soul's depths
in the world's revelation:
seek the great riddle's answer.)

There you have the fifth line representing the fulfillment of that escalating expectation that is evoked in the first four lines.

One can also attempt to, well, let me say, bring the mood of the situation into the sounds, into the mode of speaking, the *how* of speech. And for that I have formulated the following exercise. One should picture a sizable green frog sitting before one with its mouth open. In other words, one should imagine that one confronts a giant frog with an open mouth. And now, one should picture what sort of reactions, effects, one can have regarding this frog. There will be humor in the emotion as well as all that should be evoked in the soul in a lively manner. Then, one should address this frog in the following way:

Lalle Lieder lieblich
Lipplicher Laffe
Lappiger lumpiger
Laichiger Lurch

Picture to yourself: that a horse is walking across a field. The content does not matter. Naturally, you must now imagine that horses whistle! Now you express the fact that you have here in the following manner:

Pfiffig pfeifen
Pfäffische Pferde
Pflegend Pflüge
Pferchend Pfirsiche

and then you vary that by saying it this way:

Pfiffig pfeifen aus Näpfen
Pfäffische Pferde schlüpfend
Pflegend Pflüge hüpfend
Pferchend Pfirsiche knüpfend

And then – but please, do learn it by heart, so that you can fluently repeat the one version after the other – there is a third version. Learn all three by heart, and try to say them so fluently that during the speaking of one version you will not be confused by the other. That is what counts. Take as the third form:

Kopfpfiffig pfeifen aus Näpfen
Napfpfäffische Pferde schlüpfend
Wipfend pflegend Pflüge hüpfend
Tipfend pferchend Pfirsiche knüpfend

Learn one after the other, so that you can do the three versions by heart, and that one never interferes when you say the other.

Something similar can be done with the following two verses:

Ketzer petzten jetzt kläglich
Letztlich leicht skeptisch

and now the other version:

Ketzerkrächzer petzten jetzt kläglich
Letztlich plötzlich leicht skeptisch

Again, learn it by heart and say one after the other!

One can achieve smooth speech if one practices something like the following:

Nur renn nimmer reuig
Gierig grinsend
Knoten knipsend
Pfänder knüpfend

One has to accustom oneself to say this sound sequence, '*Nur renn....*' You will see what you gain for your tongue, your organs of speech, if you do such exercises.

Now, such an exercise that lasts a bit longer, through which this flexibility of speech can be attained – I believe actors have already discovered afterwards that this was the best way to make their speech pliable:

Zuwider zwingen zwar
Zweizweckige Zwacker zu wenig
Zwanzig Zwerge
Die sehnige Krebse
Sicher suchend schmausen
Dass schmatzende Schmachter
Schmiegsam schnellstens
Schnurrig schnalzen

And then: one occasionally requires presence of mind in direct speech. One can acquire it by something like the following:

Klipp plapp plick glick
Klingt Klapperrichtig
Knatternd trappend
Rossegetrippel

Then, for further acquisition of presence of mind in speaking, the following two examples can be placed together:

Schlinge Schlange geschwinde
Gewundene Fundewecken weg

The 'Wecken weg' is in there, too, but as a sound motif, thus:

Gewundene Fundewecken
Geschwinde schlinge Schlange weg

The following example is useful for putting some muscle into speech, so that one is in a position, in speaking, to slap somebody down in a discussion sometimes (something that is quite necessary in speaking!):

Marsch schmachtender
Klappriger Racker
Krackle plappernd linkisch
Flink von vorne fort

Then, for somebody who stutters a little, the following two examples should still be mentioned:

Nimm mir nimmer
Was sich wässerig
Mit Teilen mitteilt

For everyone who stutters, this example is good. When stuttering, one can also say it in the way below:

Nimmer nimm mir
Wässerige Wickel
Was sich schlecht mitteilt
Mit Teilen deiner Rede

The point is, of course, that the person who stutters must make a real effort.

One should by no means believe that what I want to call speech gymnastics, can or should only be practiced with sentences that are meaningful for the intellect. Because in those sentences that contain sense for the intellect, the attentiveness for the meaning instinctively outweighs anything else too much, so that we do not rely correctly on the sounds, the saying. And it is really necessary that, in a certain sense, we tear speaking loose from ourselves, actually manage to separate it from ourselves. In the same way as one can separate writing from oneself, one can also tear speaking loose from oneself.

There are two ways to write for the human being. One way consists of man's writing egotistically; he has the forms of the letters in his limbs, as it were, and lets them flow out of his limbs. One emphasized such a style of writing for a certain length of time – it is probably still the same today – when one gave lessons in penmanship for those who were to be employed in business offices or people like that. For example, I have observed at one time how such a lesson in writing was conducted for employees of commercial establishments so that the persons in question had to develop every letter out of a kind of curve. They had to learn swinging motions with the hand; then they had to put these motions down on paper; this way, everything is in the hand, in the limbs; and one is not really present with anything but the hand in writing. Another form of writing is the one that is not egotistical; it is the unselfish style of writing. It consists of not really writing with the hand, as it were, but with the eye; one always looks at it and basically draws the letter. Thus, what is in the formation of the hand is of importance to a lesser degree; one really acts like one does when sketching, where one is not the slave of a handwriting. Instead, after a while, one has difficulty in even writing one's name the same way one has written it just the time before. For most people it is so terribly easy to write their name the way they have always written it. It flows out of their hand. But those persons who place something artistic into the script, they write with the eye. They follow the style of the lines with the eye. And there, the script indeed separates itself from the person. Then – while it is in a certain respect not desirable to practice that – a person can imitate scripts, vary scripts in different ways. I do not say that one should practice that especially, but I mean that it results as an extreme when one paints one's script, as it were. This is the more unselfish writing. Writing out of the limbs, on the other hand, is the more selfish, the egotistic way.

Speech is also selfish in most people. It simply emerges out of the speech organs. But you can gradually accustom yourselves to experience your speech in such a way that it seems to float around you, as if the words flew around you. You can really have a sort of experience of your words. Then, speaking separates itself from you It becomes objective. You hear yourself speak quite instinctively. In speaking, your head becomes enlarged, as it were, and you feel the weaving of sounds and the words in your surroundings. One gradually learns to listen to the sounds, the words. And one can achieve that particularly through such exercises. That way, there is in fact not just yelling into a room anymore – by yelling, I do not mean shouting out loud only; one can yell in whispering, too, if one actually speaks only for one's own sake, the way it emerges out of the speech organs – instead one really lives, in speaking, with space. One feels the resonance in space, as it were. This has become a fumbling mischief in certain speech theories – theories of speech teaching or speech study, if you will – of recent times. One has made people speak with body resonance, with abdominal resonances, with nasal resonances, and so forth. But all these inner resonances are a vice. A true resonance can only be an experienced one. One experiences such a resonance not by the impact of the sound against the interior of the nose; instead one feels it only in front of the nose, outside. Thus, language in fact attains to abundance. And of course, the language of a speaker should be abundant. A speaker should swallow as little as possible.

Do not believe that this is unimportant for the speaker; it is rather of great significance for the speaker. Whether we present something in a correct way to people depends most certainly on what position we are able to take in regard to speech itself. One doesn't have to go quite so far as a certain actor who was acquainted with me, who never said "*Freundrl*" (Austrian dialect for "Friend" – note by translator) but always "*Freunderl*," because he wanted to place himself into every syllable. He did that to the extreme. But one should develop the instinctive talent not to swallow syllables, syllable forms, and syllable formations. One can accomplish that if one tries to find one's way into rhythmic speech in such a way that, placing oneself into the whole sound modulation, one recites to oneself:

Und es wallet und siedelt und brauset und zischt,
Wie wenn Wasser mit Feuer sich mengt...

(Quote from Schiller's *The Diver*)

So: it is a matter of placing oneself not only into the sound as such but into the sound modulation, into this "growing round" and the angularity of sound.

If somebody believes that he could become a speaker without putting any value on this, then he labors under the same misconception as a human soul that has arrived at the point between death and a new birth, when it once again will descend to the earth, and does not want to embody itself because it does not want to enter into the molding of the stomach, the lungs, the kidney, and so forth. It is really a matter of having to draw on everything that makes a speech complete.

One should at least put some value on the organism of speech and the genius of language as well. One should not forget that valuing the organism of speech, the genius of language, is creative, in the sense of creating imagination. He who cannot occupy himself with language, listening inwardly, will not receive images, will not be the recipient of thoughts; he will remain clumsy in thinking. He will become one who is abstract in speaking, if not a pedant. Particularly, in experiencing the sounds, the imagery in speech formation, in this itself lies something that entices the thoughts out of our souls that we need to carry before the listeners. In experiencing the word, something creative is implied in regard to the inner organization of the human being. This should never be forgotten. It is extremely important. In all cases, the feeling should pervade us how the word, the sequence of words, the word formation, the sentence construction, how these are related to our whole organism. Just as one can figure out a person from the physiognomy, one can even more readily – I don't mean from what he says but from the *how* of his speech – one can figure out the whole human being from his manner of speech.

But this *how* of his speech emerges out of the whole human being. And it is by all means a matter of focusing – delicately of course, not by treating ourselves like we were the patient – on the physical body. For example, it is beneficial for somebody who, through education or perhaps even heredity, is predisposed to speaking pedantically, to try, with stimulating tea that he partakes of every so often, to wean himself from pedantry. As I have said, these things must be done with care. For one person, this tea is right; for another, the other tea is good. Ordinary tea, as I have repeatedly mentioned, is a very good diet for diplomats: diplomats have to be witty, which means having to chat at random about one thing after another, none of which must be pedantic, but instead has to exhibit the ease of switching from one sentence to another. This is why tea is indeed the drink of diplomats. Coffee, on the other hand, makes one logical. This is why, normally not being very logical by nature, reporters write their articles most frequently in coffee houses. Now, since the advent of the typewriter, matters are a little different; but in earlier days, one could meet whole groups of journalists in coffee houses, chewing on their pen and drinking coffee so that at last, one thought could align itself with the next one. Therefore, if one discovers that one has too much of what is of the tea quality, then coffee is something that can have an equalizing effect. But, as was mentioned before, all this is not altogether meant as a prescription, but pointing in that direction. And if somebody, for example, is predisposed to mix some annoying sound into his speech – let's say if somebody says, "he," after every third syllable, or something like that – then I advise him to drink some weak senna-leaf-tea twice a week in the evening, and he will see what a beneficial effect that will have.

It is indeed so: since the matters that come to expression in a lecture, in a speech, must come out of the whole person, diet must by no means be overlooked. This is not only the case in an obvious sense. Of course, one can hear by the speech whether it comes from a person who has let endless amounts of beer flow down his gullet, or something like that. This is an obvious case. He who has an ear for speech knows very well whether a given speaker is a tea-drinker or a coffee-drinker, whether he suffers from constipation or its opposite. In speech, everything is expressed with absolute certainty, and all of that has to be taken into consideration. One will gradually develop an instinct for these matters if one becomes sensitive to language in one's surroundings the way I have described it.

However, the various languages lend themselves in different ways, and in varying degrees, to being heard in the surroundings. A language such as the Latin tongue is particularly suitable for the above purpose. The same with Italian. I mean by this, to be heard objectively by the one who is speaking himself. The English language, for example, is little suited for this, because this language is very similar to the script that flows out of the limbs. The more abstract the languages are, the less suitable they are to be heard inwardly and to become objective. Oh, how in former times the German *Nibelungen* song sounded:

> *Uns ist in alten maeren*
> *wunders vil geseit*
> *von heleden lobebaeren,*
> *von grôzer arebeit;*
> *von freude unt hôchgezîten,*
> *von weinen unde klagen,*
> *von küener recken strîten*
> *müget ir nu wunder hoeren sagen.*
>
> *Ez wuohs in Buregonden*
> *ein vil edel magedîn,*
> *daz in allen landen*
> *niht schoeners mohte sîn,*
> *Kriemhilt geheizen;*
> *diu wart ein schoene wîp,*
> *Dar umbe muosen dëgene*
> *vil verliesen dën lìp.*

That hears itself while one is speaking! Through such things one must learn to experience language. Naturally, languages become abstract in the course of their development. Then one must bring the concrete substance into it from within, permeate it with the obvious. Abstractly placed side by side, what a difference:

Uns ist in alten maeren wunders vil geseit

and

Uns wird in alten Märchen Wunderbares viel erzählt

and so forth!

But if one becomes accustomed to listening, this can certainly also be brought into the more modern language, and there, much can be done in speech towards the latter's becoming something that has its own genius. But for that, such exercises are required, so that listening in the spirit and speaking out of the spirit fit into one another. And so, I want to repeat the verse one more time:

Erfüllung geht
Durch Hoffnung
Geht durch Sehnen
Durch Wollen
Wollen weht
Im Webenden
Weht im Bebenden
Webend bindend
Im Finden.
Findend windend
Kündend

Only by placing the sound into various relation-ships, does one arrive at an experiencing of the sound, the metamorphosis of the sound, and the looking at the word, the seeing of the word.

Then, when something like what I have described today as creating a disposition through catch-sentences, as our inner soul-preparation, is united with what we can in the above way gain out of the language, then it all works toward public speaking.

One more thing is required besides all the others I have already mentioned: responsibility! This implies that one should be aware that one does not have the right to set all of one's ill-mannered speech-habits be-fore an audience. One should learn to feel that for a public appearance one does require education of speech, a going-out of oneself, and plasticity in regard to speech. Responsibility towards speech! It is very comfortable to remain standing and to speak the way one normally does, and to swallow as much as one is used to swallow; to swallow (*verschlucken*), to squeeze (*quetschen*), and to bend (*biegen*) and break (*brechen*), and to pull (*dehnen*) at the words just the way it suits one. But one may not remain with this squeezing (*Quetschen*) and pushing (*Drücken*) and pulling (*Dehnen*) and cornering (*Ecken*) and similar speech mannerisms. Instead, one must try to come to the aid of one's speaking even in regard to the form. If one supports one's speaking in this manner, one is quite simply also led to the point where one addresses an audience with a certain respect. One approaches public speaking with a certain reserve and speaks to an audience with respect. And this is absolutely necessary. One can accomplish this if, on the one side, one perfects the soul aspect; and, on the other side, formulates the physical in the way I have demonstrated in the second part of the lecture. Even if one only has to give occasional talks, such matters still play an important part.

Say, for example, that one has to give discussions on the building, the Goetheanum. Since one naturally cannot make a separate preparation for each discussion, one should basically, in that case, properly prepare oneself, the way I have explained it, at least twice a week for the talk in question. One should actually only extemporize, if one practices the preparation, as it were, as a constant exercise.

Then one will also discover how, I should like to say, the outer form unites itself with the substance. And we shall have to speak about this point in particular one more time tomorrow: about the union of the form technique with the soul technique.

The course is brief, unfortunately; one can barely get past the introduction. But I would find it irresponsible not to have said what I did say in particular in the course of these lectures.

Lecture 6

Since today must be our last session, we will be concerned with filling out and expanding upon what has been said; so you must consider this rather like a final clearance at a rummage sale, where what has been left is finally brought out.

First, I would like most of all to say that one must keep in mind that the speaker is in an essentially different position than one who gives something he has written to a reader. The speaker must be very aware that he does not have a reader before him, but rather a listener. The listener is not in a position to go back and reread a sentence he has not understood. The reader, of course, can do this, and this must be kept in mind. This situation can be met by presenting through repetition what is considered important, even indispensable, for a grasp of the whole. Naturally, care must be taken that such repetitions are varied, that the most important things are put forth in varied formulations while, at the same time, this variety of rephrasings does not bore the listener who has a gift for comprehension. The speaker will have to see to it that the different ways he phrases one and the same thing have, as it were, a sort of artistic character.

The artistic aspect of speaking is, in general, something that must be kept clearly in mind, the more the subject matter is concerned with logic, life experience, and other powers of understanding. The more the speaker is appealing to the understanding through strenuous thinking, the more he must proceed artistically – through repetition, composition, and many other things that will be mentioned today. You must remember that the artistic has its own means of facilitating understanding. Take repetition, for example, which can work in such a way that it forms a sort of facilitation for the listener. Differently phrased repetitions give the listener occasion to give up rigidly holding himself to one or another phrase and to hear what lies between them. In this way his comprehension is freed, giving him the feeling of release, and that aids understanding to an extraordinary degree.

However, not only should different means of artistically structuring the speech be applied, but also different ways of executing it. For example, take the speaker who, in seeking the right word for something, brings in a question in such a way that he actually speaks the question amidst the usual flow of statements. What does it mean to address one's listeners with a question? Questions that are listened to actually work mainly on the listener's inhalation. The listener lives during his listening in a breathing-in, breathing-out, breathing-in, breathing-out. That is not only important for speaking. It is also most important for listening. If the lecturer brings up a question, the listener's exhalation can, as it were, remain unused. Listening is diverted into inhalation on hearing a question. This is not contradicted by a situation when the listener may be breathing out on hearing a question. Listening takes place not only directly but indirectly, so that a sentence which falls during an exhalation – if it is a question – is really only rightly perceived, rightly taken in, during the subsequent inhalation. In short, inhalation is essentially connected with hearing a content in question form. However, because of the fact that inhalation is engaged by a question being thrown out, the whole process of listening is internalized. What is said goes somewhat more deeply into the soul than if one listens merely to an assertion.

When a person hears a straight assertion, his actual tendency is to engage neither his inhalation nor his exhalation. The assertion may sink in a little, but it doesn't actually even engage the sense organs much.

Lengthy assertions concerning logical matters are, on the whole, unfortunate in a lecture. Whoever would lecture as if he were merely giving a reasoned argument has gotten hold of a great instrument – to put his listeners to sleep; for such a logical development has the disadvantage that it removes the understanding from the organ of hearing. One doesn't listen properly to logic. Furthermore, it doesn't really form the breath; it doesn't set it going in varied waves. The breath remains essentially in its most neutral state when a logical assertion is listened to, thus one goes to sleep with it. This is a wholly organic process. Logical assertions are perforce impersonal – but that takes its toll.

Thus, one who wants to develop into a speaker must take care whenever possible not to speak in logical formulae but in figures of speech, while remaining logical. To these figures of speech belongs the question. Also belonging to figures of speech is the ploy of occasionally saying the opposite of what one really wants to say. This has to be said in such a way that the listener knows he is to understand the opposite. Thus, let us say, the speaker says straight out, and even in an assertive tone: Kully is stupid. Under certain circumstances that could prove to be not a very good turn of phrase. But it could be a good formulation if someone said: I don't believe there is anyone sitting here who presumes that Kully is clever! There you have spoken a phrase that is opposite of the truth. But, naturally, you have added something so that you could formulate the opposite to the assertive statement. Thus, by proceeding in this way, and with inner feeling, the speech will be able to stand on its own two feet.

I have just said that the speech will be able to stand on its own feet. This is an image. Philistines can say that a speech has no feet. But a speech does have feet! As an example one need only recall that Goethe, in advanced age, when he had to speak while fatigued, liked to walk around the room. Speech is basically the expression of the whole man – thus it has feet! And to surprise the listener with something about which he is unfamiliar and which, if he is to grasp it, he must go counter to what he is familiar with – that is extremely important in a lecture.

Also belonging to the feeling-logic of a speech is the fact that one does not talk continually in the same tone of voice. To go on in the same tone, you know, puts the listener to sleep. Each heightening of the tone is actually a gentle nightmare; thus the listener is somewhat shaken by it. Every relative sinking of tone is really a gentle fainting, so that it is necessary for the listener to fight against it. Through modulating the tone of speech one gives occasion for the listener to participate, and that is extraordinarily important for the speaker.

But it is also especially important now and then to appeal somewhat to the ear of the listener. If he is too immersed in himself while listening, at times he won't follow certain passages. He begins to reflect within himself. It is a great misfortune for the lecturer when his listeners begin to ponder within themselves. They miss something that is being said, and when – after a time – they again begin to hear, they just can't keep up. Thus at times you must take the listener by the ear, and you do that by applying unusual syntax and sequences of phrasing. The question, of course, gives a different placing of subject and predicate than one is used to, but you ought to have on hand a variety of other ways of changing the word order. You should speak some sentences in such a way that what you have at the beginning is a verb or some other part of speech that is not usually there. Where something unusual happens, the listener again pays attention, and what is most noteworthy is that he not only pays attention to the sentence concerned but also to the one that follows. And if you have to do with listeners who are unusually docile, you will find that they will even listen to the second sentence if you interlace your word order a bit. As a lecturer, you must pay attention to this inner lawfulness. You will learn these things best if, in your listening, you direct your attention to how really good speakers use such things. Such techniques are what lead essentially to the pictorial quality of a speech.

In connection with the formal aspect of speaking, you could learn a great deal from the Jesuits. They are very well trained. First, they use the components of a speech well. They work not only on intensification and relaxation but, above all, on the image. I must continually refer to a striking Jesuit speech I once heard in Vienna, where I had been led by someone to the Jesuit church and where one of the most famous Jesuit Fathers was preaching. He preached on the Easter Confessional, and I will share the essential part of his sermon with you. He said: "Dear Christians! There are apostates from God who assert that the Easter Confessional was instituted by the Pope, by the Roman Pope; that it does not derive from God but rather from the Roman Pope. Dear Christians! Whoever would believe that can learn something from what I am going to say. Imagine in front of you, dear Christians, there stands a cannon. Beside the cannon there stands a cannonier. The cannonier has a match in his hand ready to light the fuse. The cannon is loaded. Behind the cannonier is the commanding officer. When the officer commands, 'Fire,' the cannonier lights the fuse. The cannon goes off. Would any of you now say that this cannonier, who obeyed the command of his superior, invented the powder? None of you, dear Christians, would say that! Look now, such a cannonier was the Roman Pope, who waited for the command from above before ordering the Easter Confessional. Thus, no one will say the Pope invented the Easter Confessional; as little as the cannonier invented the gunpowder. He only carries out the commandments from above." All the listeners were crushed, convinced!

Obviously, the man knew the situation and the state of mind of the people. But that is something that is an indispensable precondition for a good speech and has already been characterized in this study. He said something that, as an image, fell completely outside the train of thought, and yet the listeners completed the course of the argument without feeling that the man spoke subjectively. I have also called to your attention the dictum by Bismarck about politicians steering by the wind, an image he took from those with whom he was debating, but that nevertheless frees one from the strictness of the chain of thought under discussion.

These sorts of things, if they are rightly felt, are those artistic means that completely replace what a lecture does not need, namely, sheer logic. Logic is for thought, not for speaking; I mean for the form of speech, not the way of expression. Naturally, the illogical may not be in it. But a speech cannot be put together as one combines a train of thought. You will find that something may be most acute and appropriate in a debate and yet really have no lasting effect. What *does* have a lasting effect in a speech is an image that grabs, that is, which stands at some distance from the meaning, so that the speaker who uses the image has become free from slavish dependence on the pure thought sense.

Such things lead to the recognition of how far a speech can be enhanced through humor. A deeply serious speech can be elevated by a humor which, so to say, has barbs. It is just as I have said: if you wish to forcibly pour will into the listeners, they get angry. The right way to apply the will is for the speech itself to develop images that are, so to speak, inner realities. The speech itself should be the reality. You can perhaps grasp what I want to say if I tell you of two debates. The second is not a pure debate, but it still can be instructive for the use of images in a speech that wishes to characterize something.

Notice that those orations that are intended to be witty often acquire a completely subjective coloring. The German Parliament had for some time, in one of its members by the name of *Meyer*, just such a witty debater. For example, at one time the famous – or infamous – "Lex Heinze" was advocated in this particular Parliament. I believe that the man who gave the speech for the defense was the minister; and he always spoke, as the defender and as one belonging to the Conservative Party, of "*das* Lex Heinze." He always said "*das* Lex Heinze." Now, no doubt, such a thing can pass. But it was in the nature of the Liberal Party, of which the joker, Representative Meyer, was a member, that it took just such matters seriously. So later on in the debate Meyer asked leave to speak and said somewhat as follows: "The Lord Minister has defended *die* Lex Heinze* and has constantly said '*das* Lex Heinze.' I didn't know what he was really talking about. I have gone all around asking what '*das* Lex' is. No one has been able to enlighten me. I took the dictionary and looked – and found nothing. I was about to come here and ask the Minister, when it suddenly struck me to consult a Latin Grammar. There I found it. There stood the statement: 'What one cannot decline must be considered a neuter'!"

---

* The proper form was apparently "*die*," implying feminine gender. "*Das*" implies neuter gender

To be sure, for an immediate laugh it is very good, this coarse wit. But it still has no barbs. It doesn't ignite deeply, because with such a ploy there is aroused subtly and unconsciously in the listener a pity for the afflicted one. This kind of wit is too subjective. It comes more out of a love of sarcasm than out of the thing itself.

Over against this I have always found the following to be a striking image: He who was later to become Prussian King Friedrich Wilhelm IV was, as Crown Prince, a very witty man. His father, King Friedrich Wilhelm III, had a minister who was very special to him, whose name was von Klewiz.† Now the Crown Prince could not bear von Klewiz. Once, at a court ball, the Crown Prince spoke to Klewiz and said: Your Excellency, I would like to put to you a riddle today:

> The first is the fruit from the field
> The second is something which, when
> one hears it, one gets a light shock;
> And the whole is a public calamity!

Von Klewiz turned red from ear to ear, bowed, and handed in his resignation after the ball. The King called him and said: What happened to you? I can't spare you, my dear Klewiz! – Yes, but, Your Royal Highness, the Crown Prince said something to me yesterday that made it impossible for me to remain in office. – But that is not possible! The dear Crown Prince would not say such a thing, that I can't believe! – Yes, but it is so, Your Majesty. – What did the Crown Prince say? – He said to me: The first is a fruit from the field; the second is something which, if one hears it, one gets something like a light shock; the whole is a public calamity! There is no doubt, Royal Highness, that the Crown Prince meant me. – Indeed, remarkable thing, dear Klewiz. But we will have the Crown Prince come and we will hear how the matter stands.

The Crown Prince was called. – My son, yesterday evening you are supposed to have said something very offensive to my

---

† The two syllables of the name are identical in sound with *Klee* (clover) and *Witz* (joke).

indispensable minister, His Excellency, von Klewiz. – The Crown Prince said: Your Majesty, I am unable to remember. If it had been something serious I would surely be able to remember it. – It does seem to have been something serious, though. – Oh! Yes, yes, I remember. I said to His Excellency that I wished to put a riddle to him: The first syllable is a fruit of the field, the second syllable indicates something which, if one perceives it, one gets something like a slight shock; the whole is a public calamity. I don't think that it is a matter of my having offended His Excellency so much as that His Excellency could not solve the riddle. I recall that His Excellency simply could not solve the riddle! – The King said: In-deed, what is the riddle's solution? – Here, then: The first syllable is a fruit of the field: hay (*Heu*); the second syllable, where one gets a light shock, is "fear" (*Schreck*); the whole is: grasshopper (*Heu-schreck*), that is, a public calamity (or nuisance), Your Majesty.

Now why do I say that? I say it on the grounds that no one who tells such a thing, no one who molds his phrases or figures of speech in such a form, needs to follow the matter through to its end; for no person expects in telling it that he has to explain the tableau further, but rather expects each to draw for himself the pictorial idea. And it is good in a speech to occasionally work it so that something is left over for the listener. There is nothing left over when one ridicules someone; the gap is perfectly filled up.

It is a matter of heightening the vividness so that the listener can really get the feeling that he can act on something, can take it further. Naturally, it is necessary to leave the needed pauses in his speech. These pauses must be there.

Now along this line we could say an extraordinary amount about the form, about the structure, of a speech. For usually it is believed that people listen with their ears alone; but the fact that some, when they especially want to grasp something, open their mouths while listening, already speaks against this. They would not do this if they listened with their ears alone. We listen with our speech organs much more than is usually thought. We always, as it were, snap up the speech of the speaker with our speech organ; and the etheric body always speaks along with, even makes eurythmy along with, the listening – and, in fact, the movements correspond exactly to eurythmy movements. Only people don't usually know them unless they have studied eurythmy.

It is true that everything we hear from inanimate bodies is heard more from outside with the ear, but human speech is really heard in such a way that one heeds what beats on the ear from within. That is a fact which very few people know. Very few know what a great difference exists between hearing, say, the sound of church bells or a symphony, and listening to human speech. With human speech, it is really the innermost part of the speaking that is heard. The rest is much more merely an accompanying phenomenon than is the case with the hearing of something inanimate. Thus, I have said all that I did about one's own listening so that the speaker will actually formulate his speech as he would criticize it if he were listening to it. I mean that the formulation comes from the same power, out of the same impulse, as does the criticism if one is doing the listening.

It is of some importance that the persons who make it their task to do something directly for the threefolding of the social organism – or something similar to this – take care that what they have to say to an audience is done, in a certain way, artistically. For basically, one speaks today – I have already indicated this – to rather deaf ears, if one speaks before the usual public about the threefolding of the social organism. And, I would like to say, that in a sense one will have to be fully immersed in the topic, especially with feeling and sensitivity, if one wants to have any success at all. That is not to suggest that it is necessary to study the secrets of success – that is certainly not necessary – and to adapt oneself in trivial ways to what the listener wants to hear. That is certainly not what should be striven for. What one must strive for is a genuine knowledge of the events of the time. And, you see, such a firm grounding in the events of the time, an arousal of the really deeper interest for the events of the time, can only be evoked today by Anthroposophy. For these and other reasons, whoever wants to speak effectively about threefolding must be at least inwardly permeated with the conviction that for the world to understand threefold, it is also necessary to bring Anthroposophy to the world.

Admittedly, since the very first efforts toward the realization of the threefold social order, there have been, on the one hand, those who are apparently interested in the threefold social order but not in Anthroposophy; while on the other hand, those interested in Anthroposophy but caring little for the threefold social order. In the long run, however, such a separation is not feasible if anything of consequence is to be brought about.

This is especially true in Switzerland, some of the reasons for which having already been mentioned. The speaker must have a strong underlying conviction that a threefold social order cannot exist without Anthroposophy as its foundation. Of course, one can make use of the fact that some persons want to accept threefolding and reject Anthroposophy; but one should absolutely know – and he who knows will be able to find the right words, for he will know that without the knowledge of at least the fundamentals of Anthroposophy there can be no threefold organization.

For what are we attempting to organize in a threefold way? Imagine a country where the government has complete control of the schools on the one hand and the economy on the other, so that the area of human rights falls between the two. In such a country it would be very unlikely that a threefold organization could be achieved. If the school system were made independent of the government, the election of a school monarch or school minister would probably shortly follow, transforming within the shortest time the independent cultural life into a form of government!

Such matters cannot be manipulated by formulas; they must be rooted in the whole of human life. First we must actually have an independent cultural life and participate in it before we can assign it its own sphere of activity within society. Only when that life is carried on in the spirit of Anthroposophy – as exemplified by the Waldorf School in Stuttgart – can one speak of the beginnings of an independent cultural sector. The Waldorf

School has no headmaster, no lesson plans, nor anything else of the kind; but life is there, and life dictates what is to be done.

I am entirely convinced that on this topic of the ideal independent school system any number of persons, be it three, seven, twelve, thirteen, or fifteen, could get together and think up the most beautiful thoughts to formulate a program: firstly, secondly, thirdly – many points. These programs could be such that nothing more beautiful could be imagined. The people who figured out these programs need not be of superior intelligence. They could, for example, be average politicians, not even that, they could be barroom politicians. They could discover thirty, forty points, fulfilling all the highest ideals for the most perfect schools, but they wouldn't be able to do anything with it! It is superfluous to set up programs and statutes no one can work with. One can work with a group of teachers only on the basis of what one has at hand – not on the basis of statutes – doing the best one can in the most living way.

An independent cultural life must be a real life of the spirit. Today, when people speak of the spiritual life, they mean ideas; they speak only of ideas.

Consequently, since Anthroposophy exists for the purpose of calling forth in people the feeling for a genuine life of the spirit, it is indispensable when the demand arises for a threefold social organism. Accordingly, the two should go together: furtherance of Anthroposophy and furtherance of the threefold social order.

But people, especially today, are tired in mind and soul. They actually want to avoid coming to original thoughts and feelings. They are interested only in maintaining traditions. They want to be sheltered. They don't want to turn to Anthroposophy, because they don't want to stir their souls into activity; instead, they flock in great numbers – especially the intellectuals – to the Roman Catholic Church, where no effort is required of them. The work is on the part of the bishop or priest, who guides the soul through death. Just think how deep-rooted it is in today's humanity: parents have a son whom they love; therefore they want his life to be secure. Let him work for the government. Then he is bound to be well looked after. Then he doesn't have to face the battle of life by himself. He will work as long as he can, then go on to pensioned retirement security even beyond his working days. How grateful we should be to the government for taking such good care of our children!

People are also not so fond of an independently striving soul. The soul is to be taken care of until death by the church, just as work is provided by the government. And just as the power of the government provides the physical man with a pension, so the church is expected to provide the soul with a pension when a man dies, is expected to provide for it after death – that is something that lies deeply in present-day man, in everyone today. Just to be polite I will add that this is true for the daughters as well as the sons, for they would rather be married to those who are thus "secure," who are provided for in this way. Such seems to be the obsession of humanity: not to build upon oneself, but to have some mystical power somewhere upon which to build. The government, as it exists today, is an example of such a mystical power. Or isn't there much obscurity in the government? I suspect much more obscurity than in even the worst mystic.

We must have a sense for these things as we commit ourselves to the tasks to which these lectures are addressed. This course was primarily confined to the formalities of the art of lecturing, but the important thing is the enthusiasm that lives in your hearts, the devotion to the necessity of that effectiveness which can emanate from the Goetheanum in Dornach. And to the degree that this inner conviction grows in you, it will become a convincing power not only for you but for others as well. For what do we need today? Not a mere doctrine, however good it might be. It would just get moldy in libraries. It would be formulated – here or there – by a "preacher in the desert," unless we see to it that the impulse for a threefold social order finds entrance, with minimal delay, to as many minds as possible. Then practical application of that impulse will follow by itself.

But we need to broaden the range of our efforts. A weekly publication such as the *Goetheanum* will have to be distributed as widely as possible in Switzerland. That is only one of many requirements, in view of the fact that the basic essentials of Anthroposophy must be acquired ever anew; but a weekly of this type will have to find its place on the world scene and work in widespread areas for the introduction and application of the threefold social order. The experience of the way in which the *Goetheanum* publication thus works will be essential to anyone attempting to assist in the realization of such an order in the social organism.

What we need above all is energy, courage, insight, and interest in world events on a broader scale! Let us not isolate ourselves from the world, not get entangled in narrow interests, but be interested in everything that goes on all over the world. That will give wings to our words and make us true co-workers in the field we have chosen.

In this light were these lectures given; and when you go out to continue your work, you can be assured that the thoughts of the lecturer will accompany you. May such cooperation strengthen the impulse that should inspire our work, if that work, especially in Switzerland, is to be carried on in the right way.

And so I wish you luck, sending you out not into darkness but into where light and open air can enter into the development of humanity – from which you will doubly benefit, as you yourselves are the ones who are to bring this light and openness into the world.